LAKELAND

A Personal Journey

LAKELAND

A Personal Journey

HUNTER DAVIES

HEAD
of ZEUS

First published in the UK 2016 by Head of Zeus Ltd

Copyright © Hunter Davies 2016

The moral right of Hunter Davies to be identified as the author of this work has been asserted in accordance with the Copyright, Designs and Patents Act of 1988.

All rights reserved. No part of this publication may be reproduced, stored in a retrieval system, or transmitted in any form or by any means, electronic, mechanical, photocopying, recording, or otherwise, without the prior permission of both the copyright owner and the above publisher of this book.

1 3 5 7 9 10 8 6 4 2

A catalogue record for this book is available from the British Library.

ISBN (HB) 9781784971168
(E) 9781784971151

Designed and typeset by Heather Bowen
Colour reproduction by DawkinsColour Ltd
Printed and bound in Spain by Graficas Estella

Head of Zeus Ltd
Clerkenwell House
45–47 Clerkenwell Green
London EC1R 0HT
WWW.HEADOFZEUS.COM

LANCASHIRE COUNTY LIBRARY	
3011813367532 6	
Askews & Holts	30-Jun-2016
914.278048 DAV	£16.99
NBO	

The majority of the illustrations in this book are the author's own; the following are sourced from: Wikimedia Commons: p. 16, p. 84, pp. 168–9, p. 197, p. 204, p. 206, p. 212, p. 216, p. 243, p. 260, p. 272, p. 301, p. 302; Topfoto: p. 229.

The endpapers show William Ford's Map of the Lake District, 1843; reproduced with the kind permission of Martin and Jean Norgate.

Image overleaf: A loving couple (we hope...) on Windermere *c.* 1870.

Contents

To my dear wife Margaret, a true Cumbrian,
and the best thing that ever happened to me

INTRODUCTION

Surely there is no other place in this whole wonderful world quite like Lakeland? No other so exquisitely lovely, no other so charming, no other that calls so insistently across a gulf of distance. All who truly love Lakeland are exiles when away from it.

ALFRED WAINWRIGHT

OVER THE LAST FIFTY YEARS I HAVE WRITTEN MORE THAN a dozen books which in some way have been about the Lake District and Cumbria. Nothing to boast about, really. During the past 300 years I estimate there have been around 50,000 books devoted to the same small subject. The Lake District National Park may be small in size – just fifty miles across and with only 42,000 people living there – yet writing about it, painting it and photographing it has always been a rather crowded occupation in these islands.

But now, hold tight: this will be my last Lakeland book. Please don't cry – it will upset the Herdwicks that I am looking at in the fields beside our house in Loweswater. My very first book was a novel, *Here We Go Round the Mulberry Bush*, which came out in 1965 and was set in Carlisle (though the town was not named). I did another novel, *The Rise and Fall of Jake Sullivan*, also with a Cumbrian background. Eventually I gave up writing novels alto-gether, without any public clamour or anyone even noticing.

My non-fiction books have included biographies of William Wordsworth, Beatrix Potter and Eddie Stobart, plus books about walking round the Lakes and along Hadrian's Wall. For many years I published my own guide to the Lake District, *The Good Guide to the Lakes*, which went into many editions and sold 100,000 copies. Meanwhile I have produced endless articles about Lakeland and have been writing a column in *Cumbria Life* magazine for the last few years.

During all this time, I have collected about 2,000 Lakeland books, book-lets, maps, postcards, posters and ephemera – any old thing, really, to do with Lakeland. It is paper stuff I like best, with some sort of content, which I can read and study and think about.

Which is roughly what I have been doing for the last year. *Lakeland: A Personal Journey* represents a lifetime of collecting, reading and writing, living in and loving Lakeland. I admit that in one way it has been a simple matter of clearing the decks, searching through five decades of junk – sorry, I mean *treasures*. But in another way, it is a distillation of what I like to think is my accumulated wisdom and knowledge, or at least the knowledge which I have gathered around me, groaning on all the shelves and cupboards, halls and walls.

What I have done here is to put together the Best Bits from my Lakeland Collections, from books I have read and enjoyed and learned from, letters and material I have accumulated, and also from my own writings over the years.

During this year I have found material I had forgotten I had ever written, such as an interview with Wainwright in 1978, and also the story of a chance meeting I had with Beatrix Potter's shepherd, who scattered her ashes. I have also been surprised to find stuff I never knew I had and have no memory of acquiring. Such as an interesting series of letters, described as being trans lated from the German, from a German tourist to Lakeland in 1818 who tells how he managed to doorstep both Southey and Wordsworth. It is just a little booklet, with the cover missing, for which I see I paid £1.50. I don't know where or when I bought it; I just found it at the bottom of one of my drawers, covered in mouse droppings. When I wrote my own biog of Wordsworth in 1980, I was not aware of these letters. But now, in deciding to include it in this miscellany, I have found out who actually wrote them.

The purpose of this book is to share with you some of the many pleasurable snippets, and a few larger pearls – plus odd bits of information, facts and fascinating figures, interesting quotations and descriptions – which I have picked up along the way during a lifetime of loving Lakeland.

Hunter Davies, Loweswater, 2015

1

The Discovery of Lakeland

I was walled on both sides by those inaccessible
high rocky barren hills which hang over one's head
in some places and appear very terrible.

CELIA FIENNES, 1698

COLUMBUS DID NOT DISCOVER AMERICA IN FOURTEEN hundred and ninety-two. It was already there, if perhaps crouching, keeping its head down as far as most Europeans were concerned. Columbus didn't even get to America, despite what millions of American schoolchildren have been led to believe over the centuries. The nearest he got to the United States of America was Cuba.

The English Lake District was not properly discovered till around the 1770s; at least, that's when the first tourists ventured into the area. That has been the received wisdom since, well, the 1770s. But of course Lakeland was always there, looming in the mist and rain and murk of this remote and rather scary-sounding corner of northwest England.

It sounded scary because the mountains, rocks, snow-clad peaks, torrents and deep, dark lakes filled the early visitors with awe (hence the true meaning of the word 'awesome'). It was thought that guides were needed to take the traveller safely through such a monstrous and beastly landscape.

The Romans had managed quite easily, some 1700 years earlier, to march through Lakeland, creating some half-decent roads, settlements and fortifications, the remains of which can still be seen today, though they did not really hang around to build many major forts or settlements in Lakeland itself, and why should they? They were more interested in pushing further north.

Before them we had Celts and Gaels, probably some Picts and Scots – though we still argue about their precise names and characters and origins – and after them we had assorted Vikings and Anglo-Saxons, who cleared a lot of woods and plains and left a lot of place names, if not much else.

The use of the word 'discovery' as applied to Lakeland some time in the 1770s is therefore rather open to argument, confusion and abuse, but the reason for this generally accepted starting point is that the 1770s was when the first proper guidebooks appeared, putting Lakeland on the map. Literally. These early books usually had excellent illustrations, including maps, to let us know what we had been missing and what we should now rush off to explore.

PREVIOUS SPREAD
An engraving of a view of 'Winander Meer', near Ambleside, by William Bellers, 1774.

It is rather wonderful, uplifting and pleasing, as I begin yet another book on Lakeland, to be able to point out that the Discovery of Lakeland began with books. Not industry, not art, not paintings, not poems, not towns, not castles – though all of these things were important. It was books what done it, introducing the outside world to the delights of Lakeland – delights that are still being enjoyed, and will continue to be enjoyed, till the last syllable of time, as long as the last of us has breath left in our body to pull on our boots and zip up our cagoules.

*

Did the books bring the tourists or did tourism bring the books? Who knows? But from my long experience of publishers I would say they were probably following a trend that was already there. They had spotted a new fashion among adventurous gentlemen – the sort who had done the grand tour and climbed in the Alps – for exploring their own native wild lands. If people are now going off to these strange places, thought the publishers, perhaps we could shift a few books, helping others along the way? Publishers on the whole aren't interested in unknown places that people are unlikely to visit. They leave them to lone explorers or TV journalists, who always like to boast about being somewhere really dangerous and describe the terrifying sights they are now seeing, the valleys that simply cannot be entered, the hotel rooms they cannot possibly leave. . . And now back to the studio.

*

Early visitors to the Lake District, who travelled for the education and plea- sure of the journey, included Celia Fiennes. She was born in Wiltshire and is a distant forebear of the explorer Sir Ranulph Fiennes. In 1698 she undertook a journey on horseback, which eventually took her the whole length of England. She rode through Kendal and over Kirkstone Pass into Patterdale:

As I walked down at this place I was walled on both sides by those inaccessible high rocky barren hills which hang over one's head in some places and appear very terrible; and from them springs many little currents of water from the sides and clefts which trickle down to some lower part where it runs swiftly over the stones and shelves in the way, which makes a pleasant rush and murmuring noise and like a snowball is increased by each spring trickling down on either side of those hills.

Fiennes never intended for her travel memoir, which she called 'Great Journey to Newcastle and Cornwall', to be published. She wrote it for the amusement of her family. The first extracts from it were published in 1812, by the poet Robert Southey, but the whole book did not appear until 1888, when it was published under the excellent title of *Through England on a Side Saddle*.

*

In 1724, Daniel Defoe published the first volume of *A Tour Through the Whole Island of Great Britain*. He had been born in London, and for a while was a travelling merchant, a secret agent, then a journalist and novelist, best known today for *Robinson Crusoe* and *Moll Flanders*. He commented on Westmorland that it was 'the wildest, most barren and frightful of any that I have passed over in England, or even Wales itself; the west side, which borders on Cumberland, is indeed bounded by a chain of almost impassable mountains which, in the language of the country, are called fells'.

Thomas Gray, the poet of Gray's *Elegy*, published his *Journal of a Visit to the Lake District* in 1775, and his description made it more of a sensitive and lyrical experience. But all the same, he went along with the scary image of the Lakes as a place where you might be eaten alive or frightened to death. He described entering 'the jaws of Borrowdale' and how 'the turbulent chaos of mountain behind mountain, rolled in confusion'. Gray, a well-connected

An engraving of Coniston Lake and Village by John Smith, 1792.

Old Etonian, had travelled in Europe, like many young gents of the time. 'The place reminds me of those passes in the Alps, where the guides tell you to come on with speed and say nothing lest the agitation of the air should loosen the snows above and bring down a mass that would overwhelm a caravan. I took their counsel here and hastened on in silence.' By 'caravan' he did not mean the sort we see today being pulled along the M6, but a line of tourists. Later Lakeland writers and residents, including Robert Southey, mocked such descriptions, and laughed at 'the fear of some travellers who had shrunk back from the dreadful entrance to Borrowdale'.

*

The first professionally written and published guidebook to the Lakes was by Father Thomas West, in 1778. He had been born in Inverness and worked in his early years as a sales rep., but then changed direction and became a Jesuit priest, eventually settling down in the Furness area. His *Guide to the Lakes* sold in enormous numbers and had run to ten editions by 1812. Wordsworth knew it well as a young man.

After West, the other big-selling and highly influential early guidebook was by another cleric – an Anglican this time – the Rev. William Gilpin. His Lakeland book had the pithy title of *Observations, Relative Chiefly to Picturesque Beauty, Made in the Year 1772, on Several Parts of England; Particularly the Mountains and Lakes of Cumberland and Westmoreland* [sic]. It was first published in two volumes in 1786. I know the full title because some years ago I bought a copy for the price of £30 at auction at Phillips in London. They're exceedingly handsome volumes with hand-coloured aquatints of idealised Lakeland settings. The whole object of Gilpin, and his followers, was to find the Picturesque – the sort of beauty that would be effective in a picture. Gilpin describes everything in strictly visual terms, deciding whether a particular view should be painted or done in pencil, and laying down hard-and-fast rules as to what was and was not a picturesque view. He categorised

Rev. William Gilpin: author of a 1772 Lakeland book with a very long title.

mountains according to their form and shape, their light and shade, and indicated whether or not they would make a good background to a painting.

This passion for the Picturesque, which Coleridge poked fun at and Wordsworth and De Quincey argued about, was a tremendous fashion at the turn of the eighteenth century. Visitors would come to the Lakes, armed with guidebooks like Gilpin's, and head for the 'stations' – the places he had decreed were the best viewing spots – and would admire the vista, usually with a 'Claude glass', and then perhaps get out their painting materials (or pencils, if Gilpin had decreed that it was a better pencil view).

A 'Claude glass' was a special mirror for admiring the landscape, and most guidebooks of the time expected you to use one. You turned your back on the view, holding the glass to one side, and peeped into the mirror to see the landscape behind you reflected in it, getting the sort of framed, perfectly shaped view that the experts had described. Today we have photography. Or selfies.

Gilpin was very quick to dismiss scenes and views he didn't like, while at the same time betraying many of the ancient notions of the wildness of the Lakes that he'd been brought up on. His words on Dunmail Raise, for example, are very typical:

> The whole view is entirely of the horrid kind. With a view of adorning such a scene with figures, nothing could suit it better than a group of banditti. Of all the scenes I ever saw, this was the most adopted to the perpetration of some dreadful deed.

He approved of Buttermere, and pointed out many picturesque spots, but didn't like the rocks at the head of the valley – 'as wild and hideous as any we have seen'.

Gilpin was obsessed by natural views, but he took sideswipes now and again at changes that were occurring, criticising some landowners at Keswick for their 'barbarous methods of cutting timber'. He didn't mind woods being thinned carefully but didn't like them to be chopped down wholesale. Trees always seem to have exercised the minds and emotions of Lakes writers, from Gilpin and Wordsworth to Canon Rawnsley (see pages 224–9) and those of the present day.

Gilpin was himself a Cumbrian. He was born at Scaleby Castle, near Carlisle, and educated at Cumberland's public school, St Bees, before going to Oxford. He took over a school at Cheam – an ancestor of the prep school that Prince Charles attended – and did so well out of it that he retired at fifty-three, having saved £10,000, and took a living in the New Forest. Every summer he did a long tour, to places like the Lakes or Scotland, which he turned into his books, giving the public the benefit of his judgements, marking Loch Lomond or Buttermere so many out of ten, criticising mountaintops for not being smooth or lakes for not having enough bends or islands for being insufficiently formal.

These and other early guidebooks brought the first visitors to Lakeland. Wordsworth, when he returned to live in the Lakes in 1779, often used to moan about the number of tourists that were now arriving, longing for the good old quiet days before the Lakes had been discovered. This is a gripe that has gone on *ad nauseam* ever since. Almost every new arrival over the last 250 years can look back, if only to last year, and complain that things are being ruined. In Wordsworth's case it was probably true. If we agree that the first discovery of the Lakes by outside visitors was sometime in the 1770s, this coincides with Wordsworth's birth in 1770. He could, with some justification, look back and say that things were no longer the same. Though of course nothing was really being ruined compared with what happened later, with the arrival of mines, man-made forests, hordes of tourists and second-homers. Despoliation still goes on, much to the shock and horror of the residents, most of whom are incomers themselves.

*

An engraving of a view of the head of Ullswater towards Patterdale by William Bellers, 1774.

The next stage in the Discovery of Lakeland came about at the turn of the eighteenth century, when most of Europe was closed to Britons because of the Napoleonic Wars. This meant that even more English tourists went north for their holidays to experience the excitement of travel. The turnpike roads were being improved, hotels were opening and the rush to the Lakes was soon being satirised in the London magazines and on the stage. In 1798 a man called James Plumptre published a comic opera called *The Lakers* – as the new breed of tourists were called – which contained the following song:

> Each season there delighted myriads throng,
> To pass their times these charming scenes among,
> For pleasure, knowledge, many thither hie,
> For fashion some, and some. . . they know not why.

After the Picturesque, the next craze was for Gothic Horror, and ruins were the big thing. Walter Scott's novels and narrative poems encouraged people to look for old castles and haunted abbeys, and to visit the scenes of ancient legends. If you didn't have an old ruin for visitors to gape at, you built a new ruin.

In the Lake District a gentleman called Colonel Braddyll built his own hermitage in his garden near Ulverston and employed a full-time hermit who lived in it for twenty years and never cut his hair. The same Colonel Braddyll turned one of Derwentwater's islands into an eighteenth-century version of Disneyland, combining the fashion for the Picturesque and the Gothic by building a mock church and fort as well as his own Druids' circle, based on the Castlerigg stones.

*

Wordsworth, for all that he moaned about the tourists, in the end did more than anyone else to pull them in. His *Guide to the Lakes* made him better known to many people than his poems. The poet and critic Matthew Arnold first told the story about the clergyman who asked Wordsworth if he'd written anything else apart from his *Guide to the Lakes*. The episode has passed down through the decades and become legendary, but it probably did actually happen. Wordsworth's poems never sold all that well compared with Scott's novels, but *Guide to the Lakes* was a bestseller.

Its origins go back to 1810 when Wordsworth wrote an anonymous introduction to a collection of drawings of the Lakes made by a Norfolk vicar. He had thought, off and on, of doing some sort of guidebook, and his wife Mary had suggested it to him in 1807 after they had been on a tour of West Cumberland, visiting Ennerdale, Wast Water and Cockermouth. It's not clear why, three years later, he decided to write the words for someone else's drawings – someone he didn't know and whose drawings he didn't actually like. In a letter to a friend, Lady Beaumont, he said:

> . . .the drawings, or etchings, or whatever they may be called, are, I know, such as to you and Sir George must be intolerable. You will receive from them that sort of disgust which I do from bad poetry, a disgust which can never be felt in its full strength but by those who are practised in an art, as well as amateurs of it. They will please many who in all the arts are most taken with what is worthless.

No doubt Wordsworth simply needed the money – the lame excuse that writers before and since have often given for taking on a job they feel a bit ashamed of. His sister Dorothy was very aware of the money to be made from guidebooks, and it was she who later suggested that William should write his *own* guide to the Lakes, using the introduction from the 1810 book. 'It would sell better, and bring him more money, than any of his higher labours.' And that's precisely what happened: the anonymous preface was expanded and published under Wordsworth's own name in 1820, firstly as part of a volume that included a sequence of his sonnets about the Lakes, and then as a book in its own right in 1822. There were revised editions in 1835 and 1842.

In the very first version, back in 1810, Wordsworth used a simile that has been used about the Lakes by many people since – even those who have never read his book. He asked the reader to imagine himself on a cloud, hanging between Great Gable and Scafell, and seeing 'stretched at our feet a number of valleys, not fewer than eight, diverging from a point at which we are supposed to stand, like spokes from the nave of a wheel'. Thousands of people since have looked at the Lakes – on maps and in the flesh – and likened their shape to a wheel.

In the successive editions that appeared, it's interesting to note how Wordsworth tempers some of his earlier assertions, omitting, for example, an attack on Scottish scenery for being monotonous, compared to the 'exquisite variety' of Lakeland.

In the 1842 edition he included new chapters on geology and botany. He had noticed that rival guidebooks, some selling better than his, included specialist sections of this sort. But he didn't fancy doing the work himself, finding it 'troublesome and infra dig', so he got experts to do it for him. The geology specialist was an old friend of his, Adam Sedgwick, a professor of geology at Cambridge, who was born in Sedbergh (then in Yorkshire, now in Cumbria) and who had promised Wordsworth some twenty years previously that he would do him some geological notes, if they were ever required.

What Wordsworth never knew was that Professor Sedgwick secretly preferred a rival guidebook by Jonathan Otley. 'I wish with all my heart', he wrote in 1854, 'that my letters to Mr Wordsworth on Geology of Lakeland had been printed in Otley's guide.' But Sedgwick had made his promise – and he kept it; his geological letters would be a vital part of the continuing success of Wordsworth's *Guide*.

What had slightly upset Sedgwick – and all geologists of the day – was an attack by Wordsworth in his narrative poem *The Excursion* on geologists who hammered at the lichen-covered rocks. Sedgwick referred to it as 'the poetic ban on my brethren of the hammer'. Wordsworth tried to talk his way out of the criticism by saying that it was the character in the poem, the recluse, who was against the pocket hammerers and, anyway, the attack was against *mineralogy* not geology.

The 1835 edition of Wordsworth's *Guide to the Lakes* is generally looked upon as the definitive one; it was later edited with an introduction by Ernest de Sélincourt in 1906 and, later still, reprinted as a facsimile edition by Oxford University Press in 1977. So it's still selling well. Not bad for a quickie, first written for someone else's book.

*

Wordsworth's book is a guide to his thoughts and feelings and prose style, as well as a guide to the Lakes. It's rather didactic for modern tastes, but then that was the style of guidebooks in those days. His running theme is the intrusion of man in the Lake District. He quickly gets through the touring part of the book, which he clearly found a bit of a bore to write anyway. Only the first twenty pages are devoted to straightforward tourist information as he takes his readers (or, as he prefers to call them, 'persons of taste and feeling for landscape') quickly round the Lakes. He suggests starting at Windermere and taking the Bowness ferry so as to get a feeling for the lake. 'As much the greatest number of Lake tourists begin by passing from Kendal to Bowness, upon Windermere, our notices shall commence with that Lake.'

Having got rid of the tourist journey, Wordsworth moves on quickly to consider the Lakes under more general headings, such as 'The Effects of Light and Shadow upon the Vales', 'Winter Colouring', 'Climate' and 'Causes of False Taste in Grounds and Buildings', having a go at each of his favourite hates in turn.

Even on the first page of his so-called 'Information on Windermere' he is complaining:

> The view from the pleasure-house of the station near the Ferry has suffered much from the Larch plantations; this mischief, however,

is gradually disappearing, and the Larches, under the management of proprietor Mr Curwen, are giving way to the native wood.

Wordsworth keeps up his attack on larches throughout the book. There was apparently a new breed of landowner moving in who was putting up larch plantations in mathematical shapes, which Wordsworth hated. He described the larch as a foreigner, and stated his preference for the sycamore (which had, in fact, itself been imported from Germany some 200 years earlier); he wanted native plants and trees to be preserved at all times. Wordsworth was in many ways the first preservationist, though his ideas and views were not taken up formally until the National Trust and other similar bodies came into existence more than fifty years later.

Wordsworth was appalled on moving into Dove Cottage in 1799, not only at the number of new visitors to the area, but at the new houses that were being built. When he wrote the first version of his *Guide* he was living in Allan Bank, the new house in Grasmere he had always hated the sight of but had been forced to move into because of his large family. Nonetheless, Wordsworth never lost his dislike of fancy new houses; he felt that their prominence disfigured the landscape. He hated them especially when they were built on bare hilltops to provide the occupants with a nice view, dismissing 'the craving for prospect... which is immoderate, particularly in new settlers'.

Whitewashed houses, which were then becoming common, were a particular bugbear of Wordsworth's. The practice had started as a way of keeping out the rain: the bare stone was roughcast to protect it, and then painted with whitewash. Wordsworth thought that just one whitewashed cottage on a hillside could ruin the view completely. 'I have seen a single white house materially impair the majesty of a mountain.' He recommended that if houses must be painted over, a stone colour should be used:

The objections to white, as a colour, in large spots or masses in landscape, especially in a mountainous country, are insurmountable.

An engraving of a cottage in the Vale of Newlands, near Stare-bridge by Rev. Joseph Wilkinson, 1810.

In Nature, pure white is scarcely ever found but in small objects, such as flowers, or those which are transitory, as the clouds, foams of rivers and snow. Mr Gilpin has also recorded that white destroys the graduations of distance.

Mathematically laid out conifers are still hated today, but it's strange that no one now seems to be against whitewashed cottages. Indeed, the opposite seems to be true, judging by the way they are used in posters and advertisements – a stylised country scene being incomplete without a whitewashed cottage. When did the change take place? Who led our eyes to view them differently? Fashions within fashions are a study in themselves. It's not just that views change in the Lakes – we also change in how we look at them.

*

By the middle of the nineteenth century, Lakeland was growing increasingly popular with travellers. Now even the guidebooks said that it was a place to be enjoyed by everyone:

> A journey to the Lakes, until very recently, was considered a feat of some consequence and confined to the wealthy few. It is now open to the many and within the command of a large portion of the industrious community who, shuffling off their working coil, can launch into the sweet scenes of nature at convenient intervals and at a trifling expense of time and money. In something less than twelve hours more, the banks of Windermere, where, with knapsack on back, a stout stick, a light heart, a moderately-filled purse, and the rest of the travelling etceteras, the tourist can commence an excursion to the Lakes in right good earnest and with the tolerable assurance of enjoying an agreeable and interesting ramble.
>
> *Onwhyn's Pocket Guide to the Lakes,* 1841

The reason why more and more tourists headed for the Lakes as the nineteenth century progressed was not just because of all those lovely, lyrical poems and informative guidebooks by Wordsworth and others, but also thanks to the railways, which led to a huge expansion in mass tourism.

After the world's first passenger line, the Liverpool and Manchester Railway, had successfully opened in 1830, railways were set up all over the country. The Kendal and Windermere Railway was the first to penetrate the Lake District, reaching Kendal in 1846 and Windermere in 1847. The line to Coniston opened in 1848 (although until 1857 this was only linked to the national network via ferries between Fleetwood and Barrow-in-Furness). The line from Penrith through Keswick to Cockermouth opened in 1865, and the line to Lakeside at the foot of Windermere in 1869. The railways had originally been created with traditional industry in mind, such as coal and iron, but their success brought with them a huge increase in the number of visitors, especially to Lakeland, where the steam railway services were soon supplemented by steamer boats on the major lakes of Ullswater, Windermere, Coniston Water and Derwentwater.

*

Wordsworth, as a grand old man in the 1840s, had greatly enjoyed the convenience of travelling to London on a mainline train, and to Carlisle and Newcastle and Birmingham. He had nothing against railways as such, but when they planned the first line inside Lakeland, reaching almost – or so he feared – to his very doorstep, he was up in arms. He wrote to William Gladstone. He wrote to the local papers. He did all he could to stop that Kendal and Windermere Railway coming anywhere near him.

There he was, making money out of a guidebook to the Lakes, championing the life of the underprivileged in his poems, yet when the uneducated wanted to come and look at his Lakes, he recoiled in horror, writing that the poor would not benefit 'mentally or morally' from it and that they

would ruin it for 'the educated classes, to whom such scenes...give enjoyment of the purest kind'. No reactionary today would dare use such emotive, class-ridden language, and indeed Wordsworth was criticised by the press and by some of his friends, including the diarist Henry Crabb Robinson, for his outbursts.

There's a vivid description by Thomas Arnold (father of Wordsworth's great friend Matthew Arnold) about the day he caught Wordsworth in full steam:

> My mother and I paid a morning call at Rydal Mount...
> presently the Poet entered, having a sheet of paper in his hand; his
> face was flushed and his waistcoat in disarray as if he had been
> clutching at it under the stress of fervid thought. 'I had been writing
> a sonnet,' he said. After a few more words, standing up in front of
> the fire he recited to us; it was the sonnet 'Is then no nook of English
> ground secure from rash assault?' The force and intensity with which
> he uttered the lines breathed into his hearers a contagious fire and
> to this hour I recollect the precise manner and tone of his delivery
> more exactly than in any case of any verse I ever heard...

Wordsworth lost his main battle over the Kendal and Windermere Railway, which finally reached Windermere in 1847, but it did not get as far as Ambleside, just a couple of miles from his home at Rydal, which is what he really feared. But his poem lives on, often quoted by preservationists trying to retain the old ways or by NIMBY types fearful of anything horrid happening in their patch:

> Is then no nook of English ground secure
> From rash assault? Schemes of retirement sown
> In youth, and 'mid the busy world kept pure
> As when their earliest flowers of hope were blown,

The cover of a pamphlet celebrating the centenary of the Carlisle Citadel Station, 1947.

Must perish;—how can they this blight endure?
And must he too the ruthless change bemoan
Who scorns a false utilitarian lure
'Mid his paternal fields at random thrown?
Baffle the threat, bright Scene, from Orrest head
Given to the pausing traveller's rapturous glance:
Plead for thy peace, thou beautiful romance
Of nature; and, if human hearts be dead,
Speak, passing winds; ye torrents, with your strong
And constant voice, protest against the wrong.

*

The Cockermouth, Keswick and Penrith Railway (CK&PR), which connected the Cumberland town of Cockermouth with the London and North Western Railway (LNWR) at Penrith, was incorporated by act of Parliament in 1861. The *Carlisle Journal*, recording the cutting of the first sod of the new line on 23 May 1862, took a more sanguine view of the CK&PR than Wordsworth had with the Kendal and Windermere Railway:

> On Wednesday last, with banners, music and every demonstration of joy, the sun lending its splendour to the scene, the first sod was cut of the C. K. P. R. The day was a memorable one for Keswick and the enthusiasm which prevailed was such as is shown only upon great occasions. Seldom, if ever, has it been equalled there, but perhaps it may be surpassed when the first locomotive, after whirling along the margin of Bassenthwaite Lake, comes to a stand under the shadow of stupendous Skiddaw.
>
> A railway that will connect Keswick with other parts of the world beyond its mountain framework is a link that has long been wanting in the great English railways system. Such an undertaking

cannot fail to benefit the locality in many respects. Irrespective of the development of trade and the resources of the district, which, as in other places, will follow as a natural consequence, the railway will afford the opportunity of visiting and enjoying that rich and beautiful scenery to many who have hitherto been debarred from doing so on account of its being totally isolated from any reasonable means of communication. . . Considering the desirability of such a project as this, there is no wonder that the inhabitants of Keswick should enter into it with spirit and give to the inaugural ceremony an éclat which it deserved.

The weather was favourable and at Keswick every other holiday requirement is ready to hand. The shops were closed in the afternoon and the population of the town was considerably increased by the arrival of large numbers from the surrounding districts, who have all come to 'see t'sod cutting'. About half past twelve the market place became the centre of attraction, for here the procession was to form, and consequently the market place soon became very animated and throng. There was music for the million, and confusion and bustle and noise. The Cockermouth Volunteer Engineers, with their drum and fife band, were present, as were also a number of the 'Skiddaw Greys', each member of the corps wearing a green twig in his cap. Those composed the military, and then there was the St Herbert's Lodge of Oddfellows and about a thousand little boys and girls marching in regular order and swelling the procession to a great length. There were also the band of the 'Skiddaw Greys' and another drum and fife band, and there was no end to the music.

But the most remarkable feature in the procession was a number of what the bills called 'genuine' navvies at the head of it. They made their appearance on the scene a few minutes before the procession started and caused much amusement. They were attired in new white slops and white poke caps with a red tassel hanging from the end, and were apparently well pleased with their appearance. One of them was selected to carry the barrow and placing it on his shoulders he headed the procession, accompanied by a man carrying the spade. In the order indicated and with bands playing and banners flying, the procession marched to Great Crosthwaite, the scene of the day's proceedings.

Quoted by George Bott in
A Cumbrian Anthology, 2009

*

What about the tourists? What did the washed (those of an artistic and re-ceptive mind) and the great unwashed (those insufficiently educated or sensitive) think of the Lake District when they eventually visited it, having read all the guidebooks, memorised the poems and swooned at the very thought of those shimmering lakes?

Many of them, famous and otherwise, left us first-hand accounts in their letters and memoirs of exactly what it was like trying to find a half-decent inn or, having found one, having to share it with fleas or total strangers. In the early years a stay in Lakeland could be pretty hairy – and that was just the animals the visitor had to sleep alongside. . .

In 1769 the poet and scholar Thomas Gray chickened out of staying at the Salutation Inn in Ambleside, as he found the supposed best bedchamber to be 'dark and damp as a cellar'. Another contemporary traveller, the Hon. Mrs Murray, booked into the Kings Arms in 1796 and was 'obliged to pass the night in a chair by the kitchen fire, there not being a bed in the house to put myself upon'. She then 'stayed for a week at the Buttermere Inn with the help of my own sheets, blankets and counterpane'.

Wordsworth, Sir Walter Scott and Sir Humphry Davy later also booked into the Inn at Patterdale but found the room they had ordered was still occupied by a party of ladies who sat talking in their room till very late in the evening. They refused to budge, despite the three distinguished gents standing outside their bedroom window calling out the hours of the night.

Wordsworth also had trouble at the inn at Rosthwaite; in this case the bedroom he was given was already occupied by a 'Scotch pedlar', with whom he had to share the bed. When Southey heard of this unfortunate experience, he exclaimed that he 'would rather not sleep in bed in the next forty years than sleep with a Scotch pedlar'.

Tourist charabancs enjoying an expedition in the Lake District in the 1900s.

Mrs Eliza Lynn Linton, the Cumbrian-born granddaughter of a bishop of Carlisle, was a very successful novelist in the middle of the nineteenth century, a friend of Dickens and much travelled. But she had a rather horrid experience when she arrived at the inn in Mardale to find 'a tipsy person in bed with his gin bottle by his side'. By comparison, the poet John Keats had it easy: all he found in his bed at the Nag's Head at Wythburn was 'many fleas'.

Lesser-known visitors have also given us the benefit of their Lakeland experiences. William Biggs stayed at the White Lion in Bowness in 1820 and reported how he had to eat in a very overcrowded kitchen where 'a greasy cook, who looked like one of her puddings bagged for boiling, threaded her way among rustics assembled round the fire'. The landlord, meanwhile, when he appeared, had a face that was 'an index to an excellent cellar'.

A breakdown in 1906 – but my chauffeur is soon on the job.

*

The Discovery of Lakeland went on, even when the railways themselves came a cropper, thanks to Dr Beeching in the 1960s getting out his chopper. The highly popular and very useful Cockermouth, Keswick and Penrith line, across the northern half of Lakeland, which opened in 1865, was closed in 1972. But the growth in tourist numbers had continued with the coming of the age of the motor car. Before the Second World War, motoring had been the preserve of the middle and more affluent classes, but in the post-war years motor cars became affordable for the pockets of ordinary people.

From the 1970s onwards, when the M6 motorway finally cut through Cumbria, zipping past and almost touching the eastern flank of the Lakeland National Park, millions more people – including the great unwashed from Lancashire – had quick access to Lakeland, even just for a day visit. The opening of the M6 meant that some 14 million people were now within a three-hour drive of Windermere.

It is interesting that the greatest post-war guidebook writer to the Lakes, the Blessed Alfred Wainwright, never actually learned to drive a car. He either walked or got the bus. The seven volumes of his *Pictorial Guide to the Lakeland Fells* were published between 1952 and 1965. They provided detailed information on 214 peaks across the region, with carefully hand-drawn maps and panoramas, and also included stories and asides, which add to the colour of the area. They are still used by many visitors as guides for walking excursions, with the ultimate goal of bagging the complete list of 'Wainwrights'.

By 1980, one million copies of his books had been sold, despite being published by a fairly dozy local printing firm in Kendal and Wainwright himself doing no personal publicity. Today, they must have sold at least two million. A few more than those guidebook authors who started it all back in the 1770s...

*

Many of today's Lakeland residents were tourists themselves once – and they are the worst when it comes to considering tourism in the future. They don't want any more. They want customs barriers set up on the boundaries, the roads closed and trains halted, and every outsider turned back. I remember one letter in a local paper that wanted all cars stopped at the National Park boundary and only those with proper climbing gear allowed in. You just have to look at the figures for what Lakeland's three million visitors a year put as their favourite activities to realise that climbing and fell walking are not, alas, the top attractions. These are, in order of preference: driving around the area, sightseeing in towns and villages, shopping for presents, visiting pubs, climbing and fell walking, visiting historic buildings, visiting exhibitions and museums, going to the beach and, finally, taking a trip on a lake steamer. So if you only let in those equipped for climbing, almost everyone would be kept out and the Lake District economy would collapse overnight.

At the same time, the Cumbria tourist board resists any attempt to provide attractions that are not natural to the area – such as amusement arcades – or those that will spoil other amenities. The board is forever turning down fancy propositions by smart promoters. One of them wanted to install a cable car up Scafell, as it's so hard to get to, which would be nice for the infirm or the lazy, but would rather spoil the view for everyone else.

A frequent criticism of the tourist board's attempts to lure more tourists to the area is that 'the tourists will come anyway'. They're doing something that needn't be done. But when the tourist board made a deliberate attempt in 1974 to push less visited places like the Eden Valley, and therefore didn't spend so much time and money pushing Grasmere and Ambleside, they received complaints aplenty from Grasmere and Ambleside that the board wasn't doing the job they were paying them to do. Now the tourist board people try to promote both the periphery and the centre of Lakeland at the same time.

One of the things the tourist board always proudly points to is the fact that tourism revives and stimulates local crafts and industries that would otherwise die or falter. And it is true that if you turn over the stuff in the local gifte shoppes, a lot of it is locally made. They also maintain that tourism helps farming, which might at first seem like a contradiction when you hear farmers moan about walkers leaving gates open, or about farm workers leaving the land to work in the tourist towns. But they have figures to show that the hill farmers are directly subsidised by their bed-and-breakfasts in the tourist season.

The anti-tourist lobby point out that residents don't need all those gift shops. They need butchers and bakers and shoemakers. They argue that tourism increases traffic, wears out the roads, unbalances the economy, provides only seasonal work and brings in immigrant labour. You have to make up your own mind whether it's all worth it – and naturally it will depend on where you are sitting.

Personally, I'm all for tourism. Over the last 250 years tourism has grown well beyond the worst fears of Wordsworth, but it can't really be said that the Lakes have been ruined. They belong to everyone, and everyone should and does have access to them. They are still there to be appreciated, even by those who don't understand the Picturesque.

2

Lakes and Tarns

The approach to Derwentwater is rich and magnificent beyond any means of conception — the mountains all round sublime and graceful and rich in colour.

JOHN KEATS

OUR LAKELAND LAKES ARE BUT PUDDLES COMPARED WITH some of the Great Lakes of America, such as Lake Superior, which is 383 miles long, or those in Africa, where Lake Victoria is 200 miles long. And what about the Caspian Sea on the Russian borders, which is usually classified as a lake, yet is 745 miles long? That is longer than the whole of Britain, from John O'Groats to Land's End.

All we can muster is Windermere, our longest lake (and also the longest in England, so hurrah for that), which is a mere ten miles or so long. Note the use of the word 'mere', in this instance meaning only, just, scarcely, a paltry ten miles in length. . . But 'mere' also has another meaning, hardly used these days in normal conversation, unless tacked on to the end of a longer word. *Mere* is an Old English word for lake, pond or stretch of water. The origins could be Norse, from the word *marr*, or Old Irish, in which the word was spelled *muir*. But all of these words probably go back to the Latin for lake or sea, which is *mare*.

Where 'mere' does crop up these days is in Lakeland nomenclature, as in Windermere, Buttermere, Thirlmere, Grasmere – four of our best-known lakes. Another eleven of our lakes have suffixes tacked on to the end of their names that also mean lake or stretch of water, such as, well, 'water' for a start. Sometimes 'water' is tacked on to make the name of the lake into one word, as in Ullswater, and sometimes the name consists of two separate words, as in Rydal Water.

The point of all this is that technically and pedantically there is only one lake in Lakeland which you should *ever* call a Lake, for all the others already have a word for water tacked on to the end of their name. The odd one out is Lake Bassenthwaite. The 'thwaite' bit at the end means clearing, not water.

So it is always best to refer to Lake Bassenthwaite or Bassenthwaite Lake, if you mean the lake, for there is a village – a hamlet, really – called Bassenthwaite. You would not want to get the two confused.

*

PREVIOUS SPREAD
Windermere, looking south from Orrest Head, with the Furness Fells behind.

OPPOSITE
An album of souvenir postcards for the Ferry Hotel, Windermere.

It is generally agreed that there are sixteen lakes in Lakeland; stretches of water big or well known enough to have the status, privilege and honour of being known as lakes. They lord it over lesser bits of water, which are generally known as tarns – though in fact one or two of the larger tarns are bigger than the smallest of the so-called lakes. Here they are, described in order of length.

WINDERMERE

Windermere is Cumbria's, and England's, largest lake – ten and a half miles long and one mile wide, with a maximum depth of 219 feet. It is named after a Norse hero – Winand or Vinandr – and was once a busy highway, probably used by the Romans for ferrying troops and then later for transporting iron ore, charcoal and passengers. For the last 100 years, the boats have been purely pleasure bound – but there are still hundreds and hundreds of them. In the season, they glisten from afar like tadpoles with hardly enough water to go round, or so it often appears.

Windermere in summer is hardly the best place for peace and quiet, as there is so much going on. But it is still a beautiful lake, with wooded shores and dramatic mountain views looking east and north across and up the lake. Windermere is, however, essentially a playground, with more aquatic diversions than any other English lake. To escape the crowds, yet still savour the lake, get across quickly from Bowness on the ferry and walk the western side. There is no road nor any towns or villages along the western shore. You can walk along a lakeside public path most of the way, then gaze across at the mansions – and the masses – on the other side and try to pretend you are alone.

*

In the 1990s there was a long, drawn-out public inquiry into the pros and cons of having a 10 mph speed limit for boats on the lake. The National Park people sank about £500,000 into the inquiry, enlisting support from environmental organisations such as Friends of the Lake District, stating that fast powerboats were out of keeping with the aims of a National Park, which would flourish much better with a speed limit. In the other corner, the Commercial Lake Users Group and other bodies with vested interests in the status quo protested in support of everyone's right to do what they like, when they like. The upshot was that in 2005 boats going over 10 mph were banned. Speedboats and water-skiing thus disappeared on Windermere – and on all the lakes.

*

There are still public cruisers taking passengers up and down the lake, as there have been since 1848, and three historic boats – *Swan*, *Teal* and *Tern* – still in action. It takes about an hour and a half to do one length of the lake. The Windermere Ferry runs all day long, all the year around, taking passengers and cars across the narrowest part of the lake from Bowness Nab: the crossing takes only seven minutes.

The Windermere ferry, which dates back 500 years.

Crossing the Ferry, Windermere.

The ferry is a vital link for holidaymakers and for those who live on the western shores of the lake: the journey by road round the lake is ten miles and can take up to an hour.

There has been some sort of ferry using this exact crossing for about 500 years. Wordsworth went across it as a schoolboy on his way to Hawkshead. Today, it's a motorised service, but if you look carefully you'll see that the boat pulls itself across the lake on two chains. Very ingenious.

*

The Windermere Steamboat Museum, on the eastern shore of the lake between Bowness and the town of Windermere, has been closed for some time for extensive renovations, but it is scheduled to reopen in 2017 under a new name and in new buildings.

The old museum used to have fourteen antique and vintage steamboats, well displayed. The best exhibit was the steam launch *Osprey*, which took passengers out onto the lake. As anyone who has been on the *Gondola* will know (see pages 58–9), steamboat is the only way to travel. There was also the *Esperance*, the model for Captain Flint's houseboat in *Swallows and Amazons*; you could go on it and see the little kitchen, Captain's Flint's shaving gear and trunk, and other memorabilia.

*

In *Escape to the Lakes: The First Tourists* by Robert Gambles, published by Bookcase of Carlisle in 2011, there is a description taken from the journal of a Grasmere governess in 1809 who is watching a foot race at the Windermere Regatta. She was called Miss Ellen Weeton and from 1809 to 1811 she was a governess to a family at Dove Nest. She kept a journal, but it was not published until 1936:

Two of them ran without shirts – one had breeches on, the other only drawers. Expecting they would burst or come off, the ladies durst not view the race, and well it was they did – with the exertion of the running, the drawers did actually burst and the man cried out as he ran, 'O Lord, O Lord, I cannot keep my tackle in!'

Who wants to stay at home to read *Fifty Shades of Grey* when you can visit Lakeland and see something like that?

*

You can swim almost anywhere in Windermere, or in any of the lakes, if you can escape the private gardens and private launching sites. Various busybody-ing authorities sometimes try to frighten you off, saying it is dangerous or that it's your drinking water, but legally you have every right to swim in the lakes.

If, of course, you can stand the cold. Don't underestimate the coldness and depth of the lake. The best place to swim on Windermere is Fell Foot Park, owned by the National Trust, at the southern end of the lake. The first man to swim the entire length of Windermere was Joseph Foster of Oldham, in September 1911. An annual Windermere swim is held every spring. With the growing popularity of wild swimming, it now attracts hundreds of entrants and spectators. A top swimmer can do it in four hours.

*

Windermere is home to a trout-like, cold-water fish known as the char. It is a very ancient fish, thought to have been left behind after the Ice Age, stuck in the Lakes and unable to migrate.

Only a few amateur char fishermen survive on Windermere these days, but the fish is an authentic Lakeland speciality nonetheless. Even Dorothy Wordsworth liked it, and commented favourably when she and William were served it at the Newfield Inn in the Duddon Valley. Mainly, though, she and William seemed to survive on cold water and porridge, plus uplifting thoughts. Not long after they had moved to Lakeland, Dorothy wrote to one of her aunts saying that 'I drink no tea, my supper and breakfast are of bread and milk and my dinner chiefly of potatoes'. Sounds great.

*

Brockhole, about two miles south of Ambleside on the A591, is the Lake District Visitor Centre. The building is easy to miss, despite its size. From the name 'Visitor Centre' you might expect something modern, but Brockhole is, in fact, a stately home, a large detached building in its own grounds on the shores of Windermere. Keep an eye out for the signs. Even when you're inside the car park it's still a bit confusing because you can't tell the way to the house.

In the nineteenth century Brockhole was the country home of a Lancashire cotton magnate, one of many who built imposing residences along the shores of Windermere. It was converted to its present use in 1969. In 1996 they did another internal revamp, adding a new exhibition about the Lakes.

Brockhole has excellent grounds of some 30 acres, landscaped by Thomas Mawson (see also page 28), all open to the public, with picnic spots, play areas, a fine vegetable garden (which looks as if it's private but isn't) and an orangery (no oranges, but grapes if you're lucky). You can catch Windermere Lake Cruises' boats to and from Brockhole. The building costs a fortune to run, and there are regular plans to knock it all down and start again with something super-modern and state-of-the-whatsits, with loads of glass and concrete and interactive how's-your-fathers. But it was still there the last time I looked.

*

Skating on Windermere in the nineteenth century. Will global warming make it a thing of the past?

Wray Castle, on the western shore of Windermere, not far from Ambleside, is where Beatrix Potter stayed on her first visit to the Lake District at the age

Skating on Windermere.

of sixteen (her father rented it as a holiday home). Canon Rawnsley, her mentor, was at one time the vicar of Wray and a neighbour. Later, when her books started making her money, she bought most of the land surrounding the building, though she never owned the castle itself.

Wray is not a real ancient castle but a Victorian folly, now owned by the National Trust. The grounds have been open to the public for a number of years, and are very pleasant; look out for the mulberry tree planted by Wordsworth. There are delightful lakeside walks with spectacular views.

*

Garden lovers will enjoy Graythwaite Hall, a couple of miles north of Newby Bridge, just off the Hawkshead road on the western side of the lake. Its seven acres of garden were landscaped by Thomas Mawson (1861–1933), the eminent landscape gardener and architect, who worked all over the world but lived in Windermere. Graythwaite Hall is marvellous for rhododendrons and azaleas. Look out, also, for the dogs' cemetery.

At the southern end of Windermere, near Newby Bridge, are the sweeping lawns of Fell Foot, a country park with great views. Fell Foot is owned by the National Trust, which has restored the grounds to their Victorian splendour.

*

On the southwestern side of Windermere, at the Finsthwaite road junction, completely out of the way and set in wooded countryside, is Stott Park Bobbin Mill. Wooden bobbins used to be a major industry in Lakeland. At one time there were sixty-five bobbin mills in the area, supplying the cotton factories of Lancashire. Originally they were powered by water, and then steam, using thin poles of local coppiced wood from birch, sycamore, alder and ash.

Stott Park Bobbin Mill was built in 1835 and at one time was turning out 250,000 wooden bobbins a week and employing twenty men and boys.

It closed in 1971. English Heritage bought the property and reopened it as a museum in 1983. The massive mill building houses much of the original machinery, including the old water turbines and steam engines, which are cranked into life several times a week.

*

In 1698, Celia Fiennes (1662–1741) was not at all impressed by the people and habitations she encountered around Windermere.

> Here [near Windermere] I came to villages of sad little huts made up of dry walls, only stones piled together and the roofs of same slate; there seemed to be little or no tunnels for their chimneys and have no mortar or plaster within or without; for the most part I took them at first sight for a sort of houses or barns to fodder cattle in, not thinking them to be dwelling houses. . . it must needs be very cold dwellings but it shows something of the laziness of the people; indeed, here and there was a house plastered, but there is sad entertainment, that sort of clap bread and butter and cheeses and a cup of beer all one can have. They are 8 mile from a market town and their miles are tedious to go both for illness of way and length of mile.
>
> Celia Fiennes, *Through England on a Side Saddle in the time of William and Mary,* 1888

ULLSWATER

What Ullswater has is variety and grandeur – and nearby are some of the best walks in the Lake District. If I had to recommend just one lake, for someone visiting Lakeland for the first time, I would go for Ullswater. Wordsworth was of the same opinion. He said of Ullswater that it has 'the happiest combination of beauty and grandeur which any of the lakes affords'.

At the northern Pooley Bridge end the countryside is gentle, flat, almost boring, but as you work your way along its length, the landscape around becomes more – yes! – *picturesque*. Finally, at the southern end, at Glenridding, it is all grandeur and magnificence, even verging on the awesome. It is pretty hard to avoid the obvious adjectives used by those first travellers back in the eighteenth century (see pages 15–21)...

The name comes from the first lord of Ullswater, a Norse settler named Ulfr. It is a serpentine lake, snaking its way round hills and corners and bays for seven and a half miles, but it is just three-quarters of a mile wide. It's strange how so many of our Lakeland lakes are lake-shaped – in that they are long and thin. Was it the Ice Age that squeezed them like this? Or is it because they were originally long, narrow valleys that got filled up?

My favourite Ullswater walk is along the path on the eastern shore from Howtown to Patterdale. The opposite side, where you'll find the main road, is usually crowded in summer and is best avoided by walkers. Near Pooley Bridge is a hill called Dunmallet (or Dunmallard), which was once the site of an Iron Age fortification. According to Wainwright, the walk to its wooded top makes a nice 'after-dinner stroll'.

During the 1960s, Ullswater was the scene of a battle between the National Park Authority and Manchester Corporation who wanted to extract water to feed the reservoir at Haweswater. As a compromise, the pumping station was hidden completely underground at the northern end of the lake. Most visitors are not even aware of its existence.

Ullswater is a public highway and was once used for transporting miners and ore from Glenridding. Three 'steamers' run up and down the lake. They resemble the cruisers on Windermere. And as with the Windermere boats, 'steamer' is a courtesy title, since they all run on diesel. *Lady of the Lake* was first launched in 1877, and *Raven* twelve years later. They were joined by *Lady Dorothy* in 2001 and by the *Lady Wakefield* and the *Western Belle* in 2007 and 2010. They run from the pier at Glenridding to Pooley Bridge, stopping off at Howtown.

Some two miles north of Pooley Bridge, close to where the Dacre Beck joins the River Eamont, is Dalemain, a large Georgian-fronted house visible from the A592, with extensive grounds. It's a more conventional stately home than some you'll find in Lakeland – more like the sort of grand house you might expect to visit further south, and also probably the best house to see in the northern Lakes if you've only time for one.

The house is architecturally fascinating, containing medieval, Elizabethan and early Georgian elements, as well as family portraits of the Hasells, who have lived there since 1665. There's a magnificent five-acre garden, famous for its rare trees and shrubs, and a small museum of agricultural bits and pieces in the sixteenth-century barn. Oh, and there's also a great tea shop in a baronial hall. What you might *not* expect to find, though, is their annual marmalade-making festival, which proclaims itself as the world's first. It attracts entrants from all over the globe, and in 2014 there were 2,000 competitive marmalades on display. How did Simon Jenkins miss that in his book *England's Thousand Best Houses*?

*

Sharrow Bay, a hotel and restaurant on Ullswater's eastern side, a couple of miles south of Pooley Bridge, was first opened in 1948 by Francis Coulson, arriving from Euston with saucepans on his back, to be joined later by his partner Brian Sack. They are credited with creating the notion of the modern country-house hotel – and also with inventing sticky toffee pudding (see page 310). John Tovey, at Miller Howe on Windermere – later a TV chef – came a bit later, in 1971. Together these two wonderful hotels, with their marvellous food, attracted the local and then the national quality for the next few decades, spawning many imitations and putting Cumbria on the gastronomic map.

Not far from Aira Force (see page 115), on the shores of Ullswater, is Gowbarrow Park. Acquired by the National Trust in 1906, it is now open to the public. On 15 April 1802 William Wordsworth and his sister Dorothy took a walk through the park; in her diary, Dorothy described what she and her brother saw on that spring day by the shores of Ullswater:

> When we were in the woods beyond Gowbarrow park we saw a few daffodils close to the water side, we fancied that the lake had floated the seeds ashore & that the little colony had so sprung up— But as we went along there were more & yet more & at last under the boughs of the trees, we saw that there was a long belt of them along the shore, about the breadth of a country turnpike road. . . some rested their heads on mossy stones as on a pillow for weariness & the rest tossed & reeled & danced & seemed as if they verily laughed with the wind that blew upon them over the Lake, they looked so gay ever glancing ever changing. This wind blew directly over the lake to them. There was here & there a little knot & a few stragglers a few yards higher up but they were so few as not to disturb the simplicity & unity & life of that one busy highway. . . Rain came on, we were wet.

Now for the poem that Wordsworth wrote, which was memorised by millions of Victorian children. You can clearly see where he lifted certain phrases and feelings from his sister's account – though of course you could argue that in her diary she was only writing down words and feelings that dear William had enunciated aloud. It was first published in 1807 in *Poems in Two Volumes*, and Wordsworth revised the poem for his *Collected Poems* in 1815.

I wandered lonely as a cloud
That floats on high o'er vales and hills,
When all at once I saw a crowd,
A host, of golden daffodils;
Beside the lake, beneath the trees,
Fluttering and dancing in the breeze.

Continuous as the stars that shine
And twinkle on the milky way,
They stretched in never-ending line
Along the margin of a bay:
Ten thousand saw I at a glance,
Tossing their heads in sprightly dance.

The waves beside them danced; but they
Out-did the sparkling waves in glee:
A poet could not but be gay,
In such a jocund company:
I gazed – and gazed – but little thought
What wealth the show to me had brought:

For oft, when on my couch I lie
In vacant or in pensive mood,
They flash upon that inward eye
Which is the bliss of solitude;
And then my heart with pleasure fills,
And dances with the daffodils.

If you travel along the busy road near the western shore, Coniston can be a little disappointing. You can see the lake, but it is against a background of low fells and forest plantations. This is also the most 'touristy' route, with ice-cream vans in every layby. It is quieter and more satisfying along the narrow road on the east and from here you can see Coniston Water at its best, with the Old Man (see page 103) and its neighbours rearing up magnificently in the background. (This can often happen with the lakes – you get there, wonder what all the fuss is about, trundle about a bit – and then suddenly it hits you.)

Coniston Water is five and a quarter miles long, and has three small islands, all owned by the National Trust. Peel Island featured in Arthur Ransome's *Swallows and Amazons* as Wild Cat Island. On some very old maps, Coniston appears as Thurston's Mere. It has been a public highway for centuries. Ore mined at the head of the lake used to be carried down to the foot and then transported the few miles south to the quay at Greenodd on the estuary of the River Leven (yes, that jumble of roads and bypasses – which cunningly conceals one or two nice houses – was once a busy port).

Coniston Water is famous as the scene of Donald Campbell's attempts at the world water speed record. In 1959 he established a record of 260.35 mph in *Bluebird*. He was killed trying to break the record in 1967. There is a memorial in the village. Photographs of his attempts can be seen in the Ruskin Museum in Coniston village (see page 220), and in his favourite pubs, the Sun and the Black Bull.

John Ruskin himself bought a house at Brantwood, on the eastern side of the lake (see page 220).

*

The Lady of the Lake, sister steamer to the original *Gondola*, on Coniston Water.

Coniston has lake transport services, one of which is a star attraction in its own right: the steam yacht, *Gondola*. In 1859 it was launched from Coniston Hall by the Furness Railway folk and ran a regular service up and down the

Lady of Lake, Coniston

lake for nearly eighty years. Eventually it was taken out of service; its engine was sold to power a sawmill and the hull became a houseboat. It was washed ashore in 1963 and lay derelict until the mid-1970s, when the National Trust started taking an interest and decided to restore her.

This unique and beautiful craft, now owned and operated by the Trust, has been back in service since 1980. It takes over eighty passengers, is decked out with luxurious upholstery and fittings and is the only silent method of powered transport anywhere in the Lake District. A trip on the *Gondola* is highly recommended, but not to go anywhere, just for the experience. It's best to sit at the front, by the way – there can be specks of soot at the back.

BASSENTHWAITE LAKE

This is it – the only true 'lake' in the Lake District. Although, just to confuse matters, Wordsworth called it Broadwater. The most northerly of the lakes, Bassenthwaite is unusual in having no real settlement on its shores. It is a little over four miles long but is one of the shallowest lakes, at just 70 feet deep. The hideous A66 blasts its way up the western side, but the shores are relatively unspoilt, if you can get to them.

Towering over the lake at the Thornthwaite corner is a craggy white rock that looks down over the A66. This is known as 'The Bishop'. Legend has it that a bishop once tried to ride up the screes at this point to demonstrate his faith in God. His horse, however, must have been less pious, because it fell and they were both killed. By tradition, the rock is kept whitewashed by the landlord of the nearby hotel (volunteers welcome). On the day of the Queen's Silver Jubilee in 1977, the stone appeared red, white and blue – painted by hands unknown.

Bassenthwaite can look very mysterious – which is how Tennyson saw it when he stayed by its shores at Mirehouse (see below). There is a shore path that runs the length of the west shore, though this isn't the best point from which to view the lake. The only access to the eastern shore is at Mirehouse, which has a wooded walk in the grounds. Southeast of here, an excellent view of the lake and the surrounding countryside can be had from Dodd, a small wooded fell in the Skiddaw range (see pages 91–96).

One of the attractions of Bassenthwaite Lake is its birdlife, with over seventy species to be spotted. The big attraction since 2001 has been the ospreys, which so far have returned every year. And of course the tourist board hopes they will come back forever and ever. There's a well-signposted viewing centre at Dodd Wood.

✳

Mirehouse, between the A591 and the eastern shore of Bassenthwaite Lake, is the home of the Speddings, a family with all kinds of literary connections (see also pages 216–18), making it one of the most important literary homes in the whole of Lakeland. The Speddings are in residence, but you can still visit the house: it's a homely sort of place, with a lived-in feeling.

Mirehouse today is the epitome of the English country manor house. Very often a pianist is playing. The rooms are delightful, the house historic and the setting majestic. It has a nature trail in the grounds and Bassenthwaite Lake's only east-shore walk. Mirehouse has only been recently opened to the general public and is still relatively unknown and uncrowded (it's open from April to October only on Saturday, Sunday and Wednesday afternoons). The Speddings are likely to be on hand – if so, ask them to let you hear the ancient recording of Tennyson reciting his poem 'The Charge of the Light Brigade'. There are excellent gardens leading down to the lake, which are open daily. Altogether a house not to miss.

HAWESWATER

Haweswater is today really one long reservoir – four miles long, half a mile wide and 198 feet deep. It used to be a natural lake only two and a half miles long and three-eighths of a mile wide, and the water level was just 96 feet lower. At its head stood the attractive village of Mardale, whose farms in the

LAKELAND

middle of the last century used to send 3,000 pounds of butter a week to Manchester. There was also the Dun Bull, a renowned inn. Then, in 1940, the Manchester Corporation Water Works stepped in, spent £5 million on building a 120-foot-high dam, and Haweswater became a reservoir. Mardale is now under the water.

Haweswater is one of the most isolated and difficult lakes to reach. From the central lakes you have to make a long detour by road and travel out towards Penrith. It is only accessible from the northeast and southeast sides and is in wild and unspoilt countryside. Which could be the reason why Haweswater is the only place in Lakeland – or in all England, for that matter – where you might possibly spot a golden eagle (see page 103).

In very dry weather, when the water is low, the shoreline gets bleached and looks very strange and moon-like. In very, very dry weather, look out for signs of the sunken village. Ruins have been identified.

THIRLMERE

Another reservoir. Thirlmere was once two much smaller lakes, called Leatheswater and Wythburn Water, with a footbridge across their narrow middle. In 1879, the area was purchased by Manchester Corporation Water Works, a dam was built at the north end and the water level raised by 54 feet. A 96-mile-long aqueduct still carries water to Manchester.

Thirlmere means 'the lake with the hollow' (the 'hollow' presumably being where the two earlier lakes joined). It is in fact quite a pretty lake, very clear and pure, and the woods along the west shore have a wild look about them, despite being conifers. It is best appreciated from the nice little road that threads its way along the west shoreline, through the trees.

From the busy A591, on its eastern shore, Thirlmere can look rather barren, especially in midsummer when the water level drops, leaving a ragged white scar round the 'rim' of the lake. One of the best viewpoints is at Hause Point, about halfway along the west road. There are paths leading up into the Helvellyn range on the eastern side of the lake.

An engraving of a group 'drawing the net' at Haweswater, by Jacob Thompson, 1867.

Having said that Ullswater is the one to see, there are just as many Lakeland lovers who say, 'Oh, no, Derwentwater is definitely "the Queen of the Lakes".'

They are surprisingly different. Derwentwater is square and squat, thus lending itself to huge skies and marvellous views on all sides. One of the most popular, best-known views in all Lakeland is from Friar's Crag, which is along Lake Road, less than a mile from the centre of Keswick (see pages 126–32), from which you can see across the lake and down into Borrowdale.

Samuel Taylor Coleridge went a bit doolally over Derwentwater, praising 'the majesty of its beauties and the beauty of its majesty'; in fact, he loved the lake so much he called one of his sons Derwent. His fellow poet John Keats was similarly smitten: 'The approach to Derwentwater is rich and magnificent beyond any means of conception – the mountains all round sublime and graceful and rich in colour.'

Derwentwater is good for walking, but don't bother with the Borrowdale road. For a really spectacular excursion use the launch service – there are piers all round the lake – and then pick a walk from any of them, hopping back on the boat, going either way, when you have had enough.

The name Derwentwater means the 'lake of the river which abounds in oak trees'. The shores are still heavily wooded and largely in the care of the National Trust. The lake is one and a quarter miles wide and therefore the widest of the lakes – not that any of them are what you might call fat. The maximum depth is 72 feet, but most of it is only 18 feet deep, which means that Derwentwater is one of the first lakes to freeze over and has always been famous for skating.

There are five islands – including Derwent, Lord's, Rampsholme and St Herbert's. Lord's Island used to be the site of the house of the earl of Derwentwater. St Herbert's is reputed to have once been the home of St Herbert or Hubert, a disciple of St Cuthbert. It became a place of pilgrimage, and the spot where the monks and friars used to wait for the boat to take them across is now called Friar's Crag.

The fifth island is a real oddity. Marked on the maps as Floating Island, it is down in the southwest corner and only appears once every three years or so. No, it isn't a ghost – it's a mass of weeds and rotting vegetation that pops to the surface now and then, buoyed up by marsh gases. More of an event than an island.

Derwentwater is a public highway and was at one time used for transporting charcoal, graphite and ore. Keswick's miners used to live on Derwent Island in Elizabethan times. The steamers are a lot smaller than those on Windermere and Ullswater – in fact, they are mere launches – but they go round the lake each way, clockwise and anti-clockwise. In the summer they leave Keswick every half-hour.

The clockwise route takes you to the piers at Ashness Bridge, Lodore Falls (see page 117), High Brandelhow, Low Brandelhow, Hawse End, Nichol End and back to Keswick. The round trip takes fifty minutes. It can be a bit noisy – and very busy on bank holidays.

WASTWATER

Wasdale Water was the original name, meaning 'the valley with the lake', so the 'water' part is redundant, strictly speaking. It doesn't matter – this is the deepest, most dramatic and most haunting of all the lakes. It is on the far western side of Lakeland and the only way to it by car is over Wrynose and Hardknott, or from the west coast.

Approaching it through Greendale, you suddenly come within sight of a view that has featured in so many books on the Lake District: the famous Wastwater screes. Nearly 2,000 feet high, they plunge into the lake, presenting a sheer wall that goes down to the maximum depth of the lake, 258 feet. Although it looks vertical, it's not, as you can see if you manage the walk along the shore. There is a path along the foot of the screes, but it is exceptionally tough going. It is best seen on a still, sunny day when the screes are reflected in the lake and can look frightening. Look up the lake and you'll see a view that may also be familiar – Great Gable flanked by Kirkfell and

OVERLEAF
Derwentwater, looking to the North. Skiddaw is on the right with Keswick at its foot.

Lingmell. Recognise the shape? It is the emblem on the National Park badge.

At the head of the lake there is a very small village called Wasdale Head. The Wasdale Head Inn was once run by Will Ritson, described as the biggest liar in England for all the tall tales he told his guests (see page 317). The hotel is famed among the mountaineering fraternity. St Olaf's Church, hidden in a field behind a clump of fir trees, is said to be the smallest church in England. In the little graveyard are memorials to dead climbers, killed on Scafell, Great Gable and in the Himalayas.

After Ullswater, if you have only time for one other lake, try Wastwater. It gives you the perfect antidote to those bigger, over-populated lakes. Although there are no amenities on the lake itself, the valley offers you England's deepest lake, highest mountain (see page 83) and smallest church.

CRUMMOCK WATER

The name is Celtic, meaning a crooked or bent lake. Two and a half miles long, Crummock Water is another curved, serpentine lake, separated from Buttermere (see page 72) by a narrow half-mile strip of land. They were probably both one lake back in the ancient, geological past. It is bigger than Buttermere, very attractive, but nothing like as busy.

The approach from Loweswater (see pages 72–73), going along the east shore, is a very pretty road with the lake in the foreground against Mellbreak and Ling Crags. There is a footpath along the west shore, going from Buttermere village to Loweswater, and this gives some excellent views up the valley. The lake is now owned by the National Trust, which has rowing boats for hire. There is no public launch site, but small dinghies, boards and canoes can be launched from access land at various points.

There is no settlement anywhere on the shores of Crummock Water, unlike most of the lakes, which keeps it beautifully quiet and sedate. It is in fact my own personal favourite lake, as we live just ten minutes from its shore, but I never say that publicly.

Like Wastwater, Ennerdale Water is on the western flanks of the Lake District and is one of the wilder and more remote lakes. It has a good reputation for solitude and quiet, with the result that you might meet lots of other people who've also gone there to be alone. The Forestry Commission have recently drawn people's attention to it somewhat by making noises about their valley forest trails. The valley is dominated by their plantations, but at least they have kept out the cars and allow free access. You can walk all around the lake, although things get a little scree-y on the southern shore. There's a good car park at Bowness Point, where the road ends, with excellent toilets.

The lake is actually partly used as a reservoir (as is Crummock Water), but the dam at the end is hardly noticeable. No hotels, pubs or village. The big thing about Ennerdale is that it is the only completely road-free lake in the whole of the Lake District. Every other lake, even Wastwater, has a road along at least part of its shore. So it makes a perfect, peaceful circular walk, especially for those of a romantic inclination. . .

*

Many years ago I heard a rumour that Bill Clinton proposed to his wife Hillary while on holiday in the Lake District. I never knew if this was true or not, as there was no mention anywhere about them ever having visited Lakeland. By chance, in 1997 my wife and I were invited to a reception at the American Embassy in London at which Hillary Clinton, wife of the then US President, was going to be present.

She gave a delightful impromptu speech and then people queued up to be introduced to her. I wondered if I could be bothered, as she couldn't possibly speak to everyone in the queue, and anyway I wanted to get home to watch the football. But in the end I waited and my turn eventually came.

The Ambassador introduced me to Mrs Clinton, saying that I was a writer, which showed that he, or someone, had done their homework. We shook hands and immediately I said, 'Yes, I am a writer, and also a publisher. I do a guidebook to the Lake District and there is something I have always wanted to know: is it true that you and the President had a holiday in Lakeland while you were courting?'

'It sure is true,' she said. 'We got engaged there.'

'What a good choice,' I replied. 'Whereabouts?'

'Ennerdale.'

'Oh, I know it well,' I said. 'We live in the next valley. Which end of Ennerdale did he propose?'

'Oh, I don't remember exactly. But it was a beautiful day. We'd walked and walked – and then Bill proposed.'

'Was he at Oxford then?'

'No, no – it was after we had both graduated from law school. Then we went off to England – and he proposed.'

'And did he produce a ring?'

'No, no.'

'Why not?'

'Well, I didn't immediately accept his proposal. Not there and then. I thought about it for a few weeks, then I said yes.'

I estimate this must have been in 1973, which was when they both graduated from Yale Law School, when Hilary was aged 26 and Bill was 27. Later on, I sent her a copy of my *Good Guide to the Lakes* with the page on Ennerdale marked. And she sent back an awfully nice signed letter (see illustration opposite).

ESTHWAITE WATER

Esthwaite Water is one of the smaller lakes, a modest one and a half miles in length, between Windermere and Coniston Water. Wordsworth knew this lake well as a boy and mentioned it no fewer than three times in his poetic magnum opus *The Prelude* ('The leaves were fading when to Esthwaite's banks / And the simplicities of cottage life / I bade farewell.')

A nice letter from my good friend Hillary. Guess where Bill proposed? Ennerdale is the answer.

December 30, 1997

<u>PERSONAL</u>

Mr. Hunter Davies
Director
Forster Davies Ltd.
11 Boscastle Road
London NW 5 1EE
United Kingdom of Great Britain
    and Northern Ireland

Dear Mr. Davies:

Thank you for the inscribed copy of *The Good Guide to the Lakes*. It is a wonderful reminder of a beautiful site, and I appreciate your thoughtfulness.

With best wishes for the New Year, I am

Sincerely yours,

Hillary Rodham Clinton

Esthwaite can be easily missed if you're rushing up to Hawkshead. It's not a very spectacular lake, by Ullswater or Wastwater standards, but it's very pretty, surrounded by low fells and minor roads.

BUTTERMERE

The name is a dead giveaway and means 'the lake by the dairy pastures'. Buttermere is a perfect little lake – just a mile and a quarter long and a quarter of a mile wide – which you can easily walk right round with only a few bits on the road. The views are superb, with High Stile, Robinson, Haystacks and Red Pike among the fells that encircle the lake. The early tourists used to rave about Buttermere being 'the quintessence of natural beauty'. Coleridge raved as well, writing to Sara Hutchinson: 'Conceive an enormous round basin mountain-high of solid stone cracked in half and one half gone: exactly in the remaining half of this enormous basin, does Buttermere lie, in this beautiful and stern embracement of rock.'

Go round anti-clockwise and along the north shore you'll enter a short tunnel, cut through the rock. The story goes that the local landowner had it blasted through because he was annoyed at not being able to walk all round the lake.

The lake is owned by the National Trust, which has rowing boats for hire. Buttermere village has two reasonable inns, with good beers, but they can get very busy. In St James's Church there is a window in honour of Alfred Wainwright, which looks out towards Haystacks, where his ashes were scattered. It's best to avoid Buttermere on bank holidays.

It was at the Fish Inn at Buttermere that the Beauty of Buttermere once worked – but more about that exciting story later (hurry to pages 263–6 if you can't wait).

LOWESWATER

Loweswater is probably the most forgotten of the sixteen lakes, which is a great shame, as it is very pretty. People seem to have great difficulty finding it. I am constantly being stopped on the roads around Loweswater village (see below) and asked the way to the lake. I say, 'Which one?' Then they look blank, pointing to bits of blue on their ridiculously small map. The nearest lake to Loweswater village is in fact Crummock Water (see page 68).

All our Lakeland lakes like to be able to boast about having some special feature, and Loweswater's uniqueness lies in the fact that it is the only one whose waters flow towards the centre of the Lake District. There, that's one for the record books.

Just over a mile in length, Loweswater is a nice, gentle lake, with some excellent walks on the western side and some neat parking places, if you can find them. Crummock Water and Buttermere are just round the corner, so the three lakes go together, making a perfect string of pearls. With clever car-parking arrangements, you could walk them all in a day, sticking each time to the roadless shores, taking in refreshments at either the Buttermere pubs or the Kirkstile Inn.

Loweswater means 'leafy lake', and there is a small forest on its south side containing a very pretty waterfall, Holme Force.

*

Loweswater does not really have a village, just a sort of straggle of isolated houses, but the road signs lead you to believe a metropolis must be coming up. The nearest to a settlement is the village church of St Bartholomew and the Kirkstile Inn, which are next door to each other. There has been a church on the site since 1125, but the present church is Victorian. The big attraction is the view of Mellbreak, looking over Crummock Water.

The village may be small, but the local agricultural show, the Loweswater Show, most certainly is not (see page 284).

I have a drawing of Loweswater Church and the Kirstile Inn as our letterhead. It is a genuine Wainright drawing, oh yes, given to me by his widow Betty after I had finished writing his biography in 1995.

GRASMERE

Everyone knows and likes Grasmere. How could they not, with all those literary connections (see page 192)? Grasmere is a delightful little lake. A mere mile and a half in length, and completely surrounded by fells, it's nice to took at from every angle. It has one island, centrally placed, no piers or steamers, and on the west side the fields come right down to the water's edge.

The only thing that spoils it is the 'beach' at the foot of the lake, under Loughrigg Terrace, which can get quite busy in summer. The other drawbacks are the crowds in Grasmere village (see pages 136–7) and the A591, which runs along the lake's eastern side. Lots of people stop along this road to take photographs – mostly, these days, of themselves.

You can walk right round the lake, although you are on that horrid road a lot of the way. The island belongs to the National Trust. William and Dorothy Wordsworth used to picnic there. The name Grasmere simply means 'the lake with the grassy shore'.

RYDAL WATER

A reedy little lake, Rydal Water, even smaller than Grasmere and usually mentioned in the same breath – the advantage for the passing rubbernecks is that you can get a good view of them from the road. The river that flows out of Grasmere, the Rothay, enters Rydal, then flows down to Waterhead, near Ambleside. If you are keen, you could canoe all the way from Grasmere to Lakeside at the southern end of Windermere, although the walk back wouldn't be much fun.

Rydal Water used to be called Routhermere or Rothaymere (after the river that flows 'through' it). It gets its name from Rydal village, though it isn't actually in Rydal 'dale' at all.

At the western (Grasmere) end of the lake, there are some steps leading to a rocky outcrop known as Wordsworth's Seat, believed to be one of the poet's favourite viewpoints. Nab Cottage, on the northern shore, was where Thomas De Quincey courted the farmer's daughter Margaret Simpson.

The Prince of Wales Lake Hotel, viewed from Grasmere Lake.

LAKELAND

There's a lovely old bridge just to the southwest of the lake, called Pelter Bridge, where you can turn off the A591 onto the Under Loughrigg road. You can park here and walk up the lane back to the lake. The view from the bench as you come into sight of the lake is a classic, especially in winter. Carry on and walk right round the lake up to White Moss House, then follow the road back. The 'beach' on the south shore is good for swimming.

Walking round Rydal Water can be absolutely superb first thing in the morning, especially in winter when there is no one else about. In summer it gets very busy and – for all its charm – is best avoided on bank holidays.

ELTER WATER

This is a peculiar little lake, with a funny shape – the smallest of the sixteen, in fact. It sometimes gets omitted altogether, and Brothers Water (see pages 78–9) often gets included instead.

Elter Water is tucked away at the foot of the Langdales, but you get glimpses of it as you travel along the B5343. It's only half a mile long and has not got much to offer in the way of walks or boating. Okay for a quiet stroll, maybe, but not really a typical Lake District lake. It's actually jolly lucky to be classed as a lake at all; it's more of a large puddle, really, since it's no more than 20 feet deep.

The name is rather nice, though. *Elter* is the Old Norse for 'swan', so this is 'swan lake', presumably because of the whooper swans that call in when migrating from their Siberian winter.

*

So much for the lakes. Now for some of their less famous, less popular little brothers, the tarns. It's impossible to tell how many tarns there are, as the smallest have no names and are therefore rather difficult to count. The Lakeland artist W. Heaton Cooper named and either painted or drew 103 of them in his classic study, *The Tarns of Lakeland*.

Rydal Water with Nab Scar behind it.

The word 'tarn', by the way, comes from an old Scandinavian word, *tjorn*, meaning a pond.

One tarn, Tarn Hows (see below), is in fact more visited than any of the lakes, and two of the tarns (Brothers Water and Devoke Water, see below) are as large as the smaller of the so-called lakes. One of the 'unnamed' tarns has been given a name to show that it hasn't got a name – Innominate Tarn. Take that slowly. It's on the top of Haystacks (see page 72), and is one of the most beautifully situated tarns in the entire Lake District. Its claim to fame is that it is the spot where Saint Alfred Wainwright had his ashes scattered.

TARN HOWS

It's open to the public and free, so impossible to count all the visitors, but it's been estimated that more than three-quarters of a million people come to Tarn Hows every year. It lies between Hawkshead and Coniston and is sign-posted simply as 'The Tarns'. There are two car parks, some public toilets and one of the most delightful views in Lakeland. It is a beautiful tarn, lush and very chocolate box, only half a mile long, surrounded by woods and with a path all the way round.

Tarn Hows is usually described as a man-made tarn, as if Disney dreamt it up, but there used to be several much smaller tarns here, originally called Monk Coniston Tarns. Then, about ninety years ago, the local landowner built a dam and converted the marshy ground into one tarn, with two little islands.

The present name really refers to the farm to the southwest. Since 1930 it has been in the hands of the National Trust, which does much to control the level of erosion, but with the number of footbridges, paths and fences springing up, it is becoming more artificial every year. Avoid it on bank holiday weekends and during the school holidays.

BROTHERS WATER

Brothers Water is sometimes classed as the sixteenth lake, an idea that seems to come in and out of fashion, and which would mean downgrading Elter

Water (see page 77) to a tarn. It lies just to the south of Ullswater, forming a well-known view from Kirkstone Pass. Brothers Water may once have been part of Ullswater, in fact.

A footpath skirts its wooded western shore, and the A592 road runs along its eastern side. But Brothers Water is not really worth stopping for, not with Ullswater beckoning. It used to be called Broad Water and is said to have got its present name when two brothers drowned in it, while skating, in 1785.

DEVOKE WATER

As large as Rydal (see page 74), but still reckoned to be a tarn, Devoke Water is rather out of the way and in a rather austere area, due east of the coastal town of Ravenglass. It's only approachable by foot. To get there from the central lakes involves a long drag over Wrynose Pass. Hardly worth going all that way, really, unless you're into Bronze Age settlements: there are about 400 ancient cairns and 'hutments' in evidence around the tarn, dating from around the time when the area was first cleared of forest. Still, the Millom poet Norman Nicholson loved it for its desolate feeling. The name says it all, really – 'the dark one'.

ALCOCK TARN

A small, part-artificial tarn on the fell to the east of Grasmere. It used to be called Buttercrags until a man named Alcock dammed it and stocked it with trout.

Come to think of it, to make some money, why doesn't the tourist board allow sponsored lakes and tarns, mountains and fells? You would have to pay a fortune to have a well-known location named after your business, such as the Emirates Ennerdale or Wonga Windermere, but all those little pools and becks, hillocks and mounds, mostly unnamed on the map, could be named after YOU or your nearest and dearest. Hurry, hurry!

GRISEDALE TARN

Grisedale is one of the largest and deepest tarns (over 100 feet deep), and is set in splendid scenery. It is on the Grisedale route to Dollywaggon Pike and Helvellyn, so it is for dedicated fell walkers only. The pass was once a packhorse route through to Penrith.

Nearby is a rock bearing an inscription to commemorate the parting in 1800 of William Wordsworth and his sea-captain brother, John, who died five years later — without William ever seeing him again — when his ship, the *Abergavenny*, sank. The inscription was put there at the insistence of the energetic Canon Rawnsley (see pages 224–9).

What a talented family the Wordsworths were, excelling in different spheres. Their mother, if she had lived, would have been so proud. Apart from a poet and a ship's captain, her youngest son Christopher became Master of Trinity, Cambridge's grandest college, while his son, also called Christopher, became the bishop of Lincoln.

EASEDALE TARN

One of the nicest and easiest tarns to get to, with one of the best approaches alongside Sour Milk Ghyll, with its beautiful tumbling waterfalls and small ponds. Easedale Tarn lies northwest of Grasmere village. To reach it, you take a road opposite the green, which leads to Easedale car park.

The mass of stones on the left as you come within sight of the tarn is the remains of an old refreshment hut. A painting, showing what it was once like, is hanging in Dove Cottage. William and Dorothy Wordsworth knew and loved this little hidden tarn. They often took visitors there for an evening stroll.

RED TARN

On Helvellyn, Red Tarn is one of the highest and most magnificently sited of all the Lake District tarns. It lies in the depths of an immense bowl, formed by Helvellyn, Striding Edge and Swirral Edge (see page 88). It's not as deep as it appears – only 85 feet. In the last century, a dam was built to supply the mines at Glenridding.

BLEA TARN

Say that you have been to Blea Tarn and the response from Lakeland know-alls is likely to be: 'Which one?'

The prettiest and most accessible is Blea Tarn I, in the Langdales, between Little and Great Langdale. Blea Tarn II is above Boot in Eskdale and is accessible only on foot. Rather a long way to go, but worth it because it is very pretty. Blea Tarn III is just southeast of Watendlath, high up to the west of Thirlmere. Set in a bog and very boring, it's only worth mentioning because it is higher up than the other two.

Hurry to page 256 to find out what 'blea' means…

3

Fells, Dales and Waterfalls

Unless you have plenty of time to spare for seeing natural beauties – plenty of overtime, that is – upon no account waste any of it in ascending a very high mountain.

JAMES PAYN, 1859

I N THE WIDER SCHEME OF THINGS, IN AN INTERNATIONAL knockout competition facing world-class opposition, our poor old Lake District mountains would do just as badly as the lakes when it comes to size and eminence.

It's pathetic, really, that Lakeland can only muster four mountains over 3,000 feet – and even that is a bit of a fiddle, for it is only reached by counting one mountain *twice*, by deciding it has two separate summits. The truth is we only have three mountains over 3,000 feet. So embarrassing. Still, we like to console ourselves by pointing out that we have all of the 3,000-foot mountains in England. Outside Lakeland, the highest mountain in England is Cross Fell in Northumberland at 2,930 feet. You have to go to Wales and Scotland if you want to do better, height-wise.

Scotland has a total of 282 mountains over 3,000 feet, the so-called Munros, first listed by Sir Hugh Munro (1856–1916) in 1891. The biggest is, of course, Ben Nevis at 4,409 feet, more than 1,000 feet better than anything Lakeland can offer. As for the Himalayas, don't ask.

It's actually a bit of a cheek to call Lakeland protrusions mountains, as they are really just pimples, ripples on a carpet. And yet, and yet, enough people fall off them every year and do themselves dreadful damage, or get lost and disappear, to make them just as scary and dangerous as lumps of landscape nearly ten times higher.

In fact, most people to whom something awful happens on Lakeland mountains are actually struck down by acts of God, such as heart attacks or strokes, rather than falling off frightening precipices. I once analysed ten years of Mountain Rescue Reports, after I had been criticised for saying I always wore wellies in winter and trainers in summer. Which every expert said was very, very silly. I found that most accidents were not caused by bad gear, such as silly shoes, but by silly people doing silly things – or falling ill, which could have happened to them anyway.

The mountain lump that gets split into two by purists, desperate to boast four peaks and not three over 3,000 feet, is Scafell Pike and Scafell. They do

PREVIOUS SPREAD
A view of Thirlmere and Helvellyn.

technically have separate summits, but most visitors and many natives refer to having climbed 'Scafell' and mean, in fact, that they've climbed Scafell Pike, ignoring or forgetting the twin peak of Scafell, which is assumed to be part of the same, but is 50 feet lower.

Such a pity about metres. There was something satisfying and rather grand and important about getting above the magical 3,000 feet mark. Getting above 920 metres not only seems lower, but also not nearly as impressive. However, we will use metres as well as feet on this occasion, just to give the printers some more work. They deserve it.

*

The four big ones are Scafell Pike, Scafell, Helvellyn and Skiddaw. Scafell Pike, Helvellyn and Skiddaw also happen to be the most popular mountains, the ones that are climbed the most often, though figures are naturally non-existent. They haven't quite yet got round to a turnstile on the top, though on busy days it could ease congestion, as there is very often a queue to stand on the final cairn.

SCAFELL PIKE (3,210 feet/978 metres)

England's highest, the hardest to get to of all the popular Lake District mountains, the one that has seen some terrible accidents, but the one that you can boast most about – if you honestly get to the top. It's not really very difficult, but it begins with a long, slow climb, which means the weather is quite likely to be different at the top – usually worse – so come well prepared with stout footwear, some extra warmth and good rainwear.

Scafell Pike is part of a range of peaks known as the Scafell Pikes, which you have to work your way over or around before you finally start climbing the big one. Hence the relatively long time needed to get to the top, compared with some other mountains that happen to be much nearer civilisation or parking. That's what makes Scafell all the more special.

SCAFELL AND WASTWATER

LAKELAND

A ravine called Piers Gill is the most dangerous part. In 1921, someone fell down it, breaking both ankles, and lay at the bottom for eighteen days. He was finally found, having landed near a pool of water, which had kept him alive.

The round trip, depending on what route you take, should take about six hours. The actual summit is not very exciting or pretty, being rather bleak and barren, but on a clear day the views are sensational. On the way back, if the day is clear and you feel confident, head for Borrowdale by coming down via Sprinkling Tarn. On a hot day, celebrate with a dip in the marvellous ice-green marble water at Stockley Bridge.

*

Samuel Taylor Coleridge climbed Scafell in 1802, all on his own, without a guide or companion, carrying a pen and a portable inkwell. He wrote a letter at the top to the woman he was besotted with, Sara Hutchinson, the sister of Wordsworth's wife, despite having his own wife and family.

His letter is thought to be the first recorded climb of Scafell. Obviously others must have done it before him, such as shepherds, but they never wrote letters about it. Coleridge then hurried down, any old way, ignoring all the easy paths, which is not to be recommended. He wrote to Sara Hutchinson:

> There is one sort of gambling to which I am addicted. It is this. When I find it convenient to descend from a mountain I am too confident and too indolent to look around about and wind about till I find a track or other symptoms of safety; but where it is first possible to descend, there I go – relying upon fortune for how far down the possibility will continue.

Many of Coleridge's one-man expeditions lasted up to nine days, such as his 1802 climb. He described what he was taking with him:

A postcard of a snow-covered Scafell, above Wastwater.

A shirt, cravat, 2 pairs of stockings, a little paper and half a dozen pens, a German book (Voss's poems) & a little sugar and tea, with my night cap packed up in my natty green oil-skin, neatly squared, and put into my net knapsack on my back and the besom stick in my hand.

Note the use of the word 'natty', which I had always assumed was a 1950s expression.

HELVELLYN (3,118 feet/950 metres)

Often considered the finest of the big four by Lakeland experts, for its brilliant views and exciting summit, Helvellyn is also in some ways the most dangerous – it certainly seems to be the scene of more accidents than any other Lakeland mountain. But Wordsworth managed to climb it safely at the age of seventy. Makes you sick.

Striding Edge is narrow and involves a bit of scrambling, but this can be avoided by using the path a little lower down. Red Tarn is on the right (see page 80). It gets its name because when the sun rises the tarn appears dark red in colour. It's traditional to watch the sunrise from the summit of Helvellyn on Midsummer's Day – there are always a lot of people there, but it's worth the trip.

*

A sign that Helvellyn has always been a dodgy, dangerous mountain is the number of monuments scattered on its slopes to those who have come a cropper while climbing it.

The best known is the Charles Gough Memorial, which is on the top of Helvellyn, overlooking Red Tarn. It became famous in literature and legend, but more for Gough's dog than his master. Charles Gough and his dog (a terrier bitch called Foxey) had set off from Skipton in Yorkshire in the spring

Striding Edge, Helvellyn, with Red Tarn to its right.

of 1805 and were attempting to walk over Helvellyn via Striding Edge. A sudden flurry of snow had hidden the path he was trying to follow and he fell onto some rocks and was killed. But his faithful dog remained by his body. Foxey would be found – still alive – beside her dead master three months later.

This act of devotion captivated the country, and both Wordsworth and Walter Scott wrote about it – Wordsworth in his poem 'Fidelity', and Scott in his poem 'Helvellyn'. Wordsworth's effort concludes with the words:

> The Dog, which still was hovering nigh,
> Repeating the same timid cry,
> This Dog, had been through three months' space
> A dweller in that savage place.
> . . .
> How nourish'd here through such long time
> He knows, who gave that love sublime,
> And gave that strength of feeling, great
> Above all human estimate.

But how on earth did Foxey survive for all those months? That was what many people wondered. Did she eat rabbits, birds, lambs? When it was revealed that the flesh on poor old Gough's legs had been eaten away, leaving only the bones, it was suggested that the faithful dog had in fact eaten her master in order to survive. Shock horror.

Canon Rawnsley, in his book *Literary Associations of the English Lakes*, disputed this notion and said that the dog must have eaten grass. During her vigil by Gough's dead body she had given birth to pups – all of which had died. It was Canon Rawnsley who was mainly responsible for the memorial being erected in 1891. It carried some verse from Wordsworth's 'Fidelity' and the initials H. D. R. – for Rawnsley – can be seen at the bottom of the stone.

*

There are two other memorial stones on Helvellyn. One is to the memory of a local man, Robert Dixon, who died in 1858 while following the Patterdale Hounds over Helvellyn.

The other, like the Gough memorial, became well known nationally, at least in aviation circles, as it marks the first landing on any English mountain of an airplane. On 22 December 1926, two daredevil amateur pilots, John Leeming and Bert Hinkler, took off from Woodford, Cheshire, in an Avro 585 Gosport. They had attempted the flight twice before and given up because of bad weather – December is not the ideal time to attempt any Lakeland mountains – but this time Leeming and Hinkler managed to land on the top. They got out, looked around, then grabbed a passing climber and asked him to sign a piece of paper verifying that they had landed on top of the mountain. They then flew back safely to Woodford.

*

William Wordsworth always boasted that he had climbed Helvellyn at the age of seventy (see pages 176–99). Would that he were living at this hour, or at least in July 1999. That was when William Barnes of Brampton, a retired police officer, climbed Great Gable – on the day before his ninetieth birthday.

SKIDDAW (3,053 feet/931 metres)

There are clever folks, the real climbing types, who are rather scornful about Skiddaw, dismissing it as easy-peasy, nowt more than a stroll, with no hairy or horrible bits where you can break your legs. All true. It is rather a cuddly, rounded, modest sort of mountain, but it makes an excellent mountain walk all the same. How nice not to walk in fear and dread. How reassuring to think that even if the mist comes down or it grows dark, you should be perfectly safe. Just follow the crowds.

Skiddaw was the first popular mountain climb in Lakeland, and that lovely open path from the Keswick side has been used by millions for over

Keswick & Skiddaw.

150 years. You could probably take a pram up it. In the last war, motorbikes and army vehicles went up it, no bother. No wonder Wordsworth and Southey took their respective families there for a bonfire party to celebrate Waterloo (see below). And it's terribly easy to find a place to park here, whether for a coach and horses in Wordsworth's day or for a motor car or bicycle today.

Skiddaw dominates the Northern Fells, a big brother to its surrounding mountain mass, a landmark for miles around. People who live beyond it describe themselves as living at the 'Back o' Skiddaw'.

If you go up from Dash Falls, look out for Skiddaw House, an amazing building, stuck literally in the middle of nowhere, which was once used by shepherds and was recently converted into a youth hostel. It provides good shelter in bad weather.

*

Perhaps the most fun-sounding ascent of Skiddaw involved a banquet at the top, which took place on Monday, 21 August 1815 (unless, of course, you happened to be one of the baggage handlers, carting up all the vitals). This was when Wordsworth, Southey and his friends celebrated the British victory at Waterloo on top of Skiddaw. Two days later Southey wrote about it to his brother, Harry. (The James Boswell mentioned is not the biographer of Samuel Johnson but his son, also called James.)

> Monday, the 21st August, was not a more remarkable day in your life than it was in that of my neighbour, Skiddaw, who is a much older personage. The weather served for our bonfire, and never, I believe, was such an assemblage upon such a spot. To my utter astonishment, Lord Sunderlin rode up, and Lady S., who endeavoured to dissuade me from going as a thing too dangerous, joined the walking party. Wordsworth, with his wife, sister, and eldest boy, came over on purpose. James Boswell arrived that morning at the Sunderlins. Edith,

A view of Keswick sitting beneath Skiddaw.

Edith May and Herbert were my convoy, with our three maid-servants, some of our neighbours, some adventurous Lakers, and Messrs. Rag, Tag, and Bobtail made up the rest of the assembly.

We roasted beef and boiled plum-puddings there; sang 'God Save the King' round the most furious body of flaming tar-barrels that I ever saw; drank a huge wooden bowl of punch; fired cannon at every health with three times three, and rolled large blazing balls of tow and turpentine down the steep side of the mountain. The effect was grand beyond imagination. We formed a huge circle round the most intense light, and behind us was an immeasurable arch of the most intense darkness, for our bonfire fairly cut out the moon.

The only mishap which occurred will make a famous anecdote in the life of a great poet, if James Boswell, after the example of his father, keepeth a diary of the sayings of remarkable men. When we were craving for the punch, a cry went forth that the kettle had been knocked over, with all the boiling water! The persons about the fire declared it was one of the gentlemen – they did not know his name, but he had a red cloak on; they pointed him out in the circle. The red cloak (a maroon one of Edith's) identified him; Wordsworth had got hold of it and was equipped like a Spanish Don – by no means the worst figure in the company. He had committed the fatal faux pas and thought to slink off undiscovered. But as soon as, in my inquiries concerning punch, I learnt his guilt, I went round to all our party, and communicated the discovery, and getting them about him, I punished him by singing a parody, which they all joined in: ''Twas you that kicked the kettle down! 'Twas you, Sir, you!'

The consequences were, that we took all the cold water upon the summit to supply our loss. Our myrmidons and Messrs. Rag and Co. had, therefore, none for their grog; they necessarily drank the rum pure; and you, who are physician to the Middlesex Hospital, are doubtless acquainted with the manner in which alcohol acts upon the nervous system. All our torches were lit at once by this mad company, and our way down the hill was marked by a track of fire, from flambeaux dropping the pitch, tarred ropes, etc. One fellow was so drunk that his companions placed him upon a horse, with his face to the tail, to bring him down, themselves being just sober enough to guide and hold him on. Down, however, we all got safely by midnight: and nobody, from the old Lord of seventy-seven to my son Herbert, is the worse for the toil of the day, though we were eight hours from the time we set out till we reached home.

From Charles Cuthbert Southey's
The Life and Correspondence of Robert Southey, 1850

*

One of the many visitors to Lakeland, attracted by the Lake Poets, was John Keats. He visited in 1818 and on 29 June wrote to his brother:

We went to bed rather fatigued, but not so much so as to hinder us getting up this morning to mount Skiddaw. It promised all along to be fair and we fagged and tugged nearly to the top, when, at half-past six, there came a mist upon us and shut out the view; we did not, however, lose anything by it: we were high enough without mist to see the coast of Scotland, the Irish Sea, the hills beyond Lancaster, and nearly all the larger ones of Cumberland and West-morland, particularly Helvellyn and Scawfell. It grew colder and colder as we ascended and we were glad, at about three parts of the way, to taste a little rum which the Guide brought with him, mixed, mind ye, with mountain water. I took two glasses going and one returning. It is about six miles from where I am writing to the top. So we have walked ten miles before breakfast today. We went up with two others, very good sort of fellows; all felt, on arising into the cold air, that same elevation which a cold bath gives one. I felt as if I were going to a tournament.

John Keats, 1819

*

Apart from the three/four mountains over 3,000 feet, which are worth climbing so you can boast about having done so, there are six other big Lakeland mountains, all of them popular with climbers and hardy walkers.

GREAT GABLE (2,949 feet/899 metres)

Great Gable is steep-sided and craggy, and dominates the heads of the valleys of Ennerdale, Borrowdale and Wasdale. Coleridge (who sometimes called the mountain Great Gavel; see page 102) described the mountain in a letter to Humphry Davy on 10 October 1800:

> The darkness vanished as if by enchantment; far off, far, far off to the south, the mountains of Glaramara and Great Gable and their family appeared distinct, in deepest, sablest blue.

In June 1886, Walter Parry Haskett-Smith (1857–1946) climbed Napes Needle – the first ascent of this almost perpendicular rock, which is on a flank of Great Gable. He wrote about his climb, and wrote guides to other climbs, and is regarded as the father of rock climbing as a sport in Britain. Here is his account of 'The First Ascent of Napes Needle', which appeared in *Journal of the Fell and Rock Climbing Club of the English Lake District* in 1914.

> One day in the early Eighties, the weather was beginning to clear after two or three days of southerly gale, but across the path to Sty Head only the lower screes were visible and Great Gable was

Climbers atop Needle Rock on Great Gable.

completely concealed. Suddenly, however, the mist grew thinner and it became just possible to locate the Napes. Then they were swallowed up again, but a moment later the outermost curtain of mist seemed to be drawn aside and one of the fitful gleams of sunshine fell on a slender pinnacle of rock, standing out against the background of cloud without a sign of any other rock near it and appearing to shoot up for 200–300 feet.

The vision did not last more than a minute or two and we all thought our eyes had been tricked, as indeed to a certain extent they had been, but resolved to take an early opportunity of hunting down the mysterious rock. . .

I forgot my headache and began to examine the Needle itself. A deep crack offered a very obvious route for the first stage, but the middle portion of this crack was decidedly difficult, being at the same time blocked with stones and turf.

From the top of the crack there is no trouble to reach the shoulder whence the final stage may be studied at ease. The summit is near, being, as they say in transatlantic cities, 'only two blocks away', but those same blocks are set one upon the other and the stability of the top one looks very doubtful. My first care was to get two or three stones and test the flatness of the summit by seeing whether any thrown up could be induced to lodge. If it did, that would be an indication of a moderately flat top and would hold out hopes of the edge being found not too much rounded to afford a good grip for the fingers. Out of three missiles one consented to stay and thereby encouraged me to start, feeling as small as a mouse climbing a milestone.

Gently and cautiously transferring my weight, I reached up with my right hand and at last was able to feel the edge and prove it to be, not smooth and rounded as it might have been, but a flat and satisfactory grip. My first thought on reaching the top was one of regret that my friends should have missed by a few hours such a day's climbing, three new things and all good: my next was one of wonder whether getting down again would not prove far more awkward than getting up!

Hanging by the hands and feeling with the toes for the protuberance provided an anxious moment, but the rest went easily enough, though it must be confessed that it was an undoubted satisfaction to stand once more on solid ground below and look up at my handkerchief fluttering in the breeze.

Haskett-Smith was educated at to Eton and Oxford, where he read law, but was known mainly for his athletic ability. He once managed 25 feet practising the long jump, which was an unofficial world record at the time. He never used ropes or crampons or spikes when climbing, relying on his bare hands and athletic agility. In 1936, on the fiftieth anniversary of his historic ascent, he again climbed the Needle, aged seventy-seven. A large crowd of well-wishers shouted up to him from the base of the climb, 'Tell us a story!' 'There is no other story,' he replied. 'This is the top storey.'

BOWFELL (2,960 feet/902 metres)

Bowfell is at the head of Langdale, Eskdale and Langstrath (a branch of Borrowdale). You can reach the summit via a ridge called the Band. To the northwestern side of the mountain is a pass called Ore Gap, which is so called because it is rich in haematite, which stains the rocks red. The Barrow-born Harry Griffin, who wrote book after book in celebration of Lakeland and contributed to the *Guardian*'s Country Diary for more than half a century, thought the view from the top was one of the best in the Lakes:

Bowfell is undoubtedly one of the finest mountains in Lakeland – a shy but shapely pyramid, without notoriety or glamour, stuck right in the centre of some of the best country in England. An

ROCK CLIMBING IN LAKELAND

The man above (pointing to the hydroplane): "Reckless beggar! That's what I call 'Asking for it.'"

honest mountain devoid of guile, you might say – unless you happen to be using a compass near Ore Gap. . .

The mountain is easy to recognise because, unlike most Lakeland peaks, its summit has the traditional shape – an equilateral triangle. If you ask a child to draw a mountain it will show you something like the top of Bowfell. . .

If you pick the right day the view from the summit of Bowfell can be unequalled in Lakeland. Scotland can sometimes be seen and often the Solway Firth, the estuaries of the Esk and the Duddon, the Northern Pennines and the Yorkshire hills and almost all the mountains in Lakeland.

A. H. Griffin, *The Roof of England*, 1968

✳

The word 'fell' comes from an Old Norse word, *fjall* (see also page 256). In the North of England it used to indicate an area of uncultivated high ground used for grazing, as in fell ponies. But 'fells' are also the mountains and hills of Lakeland and the Pennines, and the word crops up in names like Bowfell (see above), Harter Fell in Eskdale (649 metres/2,129 ft), Loughrigg Fell between Grasmere and Windermere (1,101 ft/336 metres) or Carrock Fell (2,169 ft/661 metres), northeast of Keswick and much loved by Wainwright. All of Wainwright's *Pictorial Guides* of course used the word 'fell' in their titles: *The Eastern Fells*, *The Central Fells* and so on.

You get the odd fell in Scotland, too, but fell is very much a North of England and Lakeland word, redolent of barren tops and sweeping views.

✳

James Payn, writing in his *Handbook to the English Lakes* (1859), had a surprising piece of advice for the aspiring fell-walker:

Rock-climbing fun in Lakeland.

We are now going to give a very heterodox piece of advice, but it is one that is founded upon a long experience of Lakeland and other mountain districts. Unless you have plenty of time to spare for seeing natural beauties – plenty of overtime, that is – upon no account waste any of it in ascending a very high mountain. The fatigue, to persons of average strength and ordinary habits, is in much over-proportion to the advantage in any case, while, in nine cases (at least) out of ten, in this part of the country a day sufficiently clear for seeing any great extent of prospect does not occur. There is, of course, some satisfaction in designating more prudent persons as 'coddles' and 'muffs', but you can do that in a very superior manner (with a little confidence) without having earned the right of insult by any such exertions. A much lower and more easily attained elevation has often a prospect nearly as extensive and infinitely more distinct.

PILLAR (2,927 feet/892 metres)

Pillar is in the western Lake District, rising above Ennerdale, southwest of Keswick. A huge cliff on the north side of the summit is noted for its rock climbs. Samuel Taylor Coleridge, writing to Sara Hutchinson from the top of Scafell on 5 August 1802, was impressed:

> The mountains at the head of this lake [Ennerdale Water] and Wast-dale are the Monsters of the Country, bare bleak heads, evermore doing deeds of darkness, weather-plots, and storm-conspiracies in the clouds. Their names are Herd House, Bowness, Wha Head, Great Gavel [Great Gable], the Steeple, the Pillar and Seat Allian [Seatallan].

BLENCATHRA (2,847 feet/868 metres)

Blencathra is in the northern Lakes, to the east of Skiddaw, and has no fewer than six separate fell tops. For years the mountain appeared on Ordnance

Survey maps as 'Saddleback' (owing to its shape), but in recent years it has appeared as 'Saddleback or Blencathra'. Blencathra is a Celtic name, probably meaning 'summit of the seat-like mountain'. A popular route to the summit of Blencathra is via Sharp Edge, a knife-edged ridge on the eastern side of the mountain. But do mind how you go – according to Coleridge, the winds on 'stern Blencathra's perilous height... are tyrannous and strong'.

HIGH STREET (2,718 feet/829 metres)

High Street is a remote fell in the far eastern part of the Lake District National Park. The mountain is named for the Roman road running along its summit ridge, which leads from Troutbeck to Penrith. Bonnie Prince Charlie's army used the road in the 1745 Jacobite Rising.

The flat summit of the fell is known as Racecourse Hill, and summer fairs were held here in the eighteenth and nineteenth centuries. Those who ascend High Street from Mardale Head, at the southern end of Haweswater (see pages 61–2), might possibly be rewarded by the sight of England's only golden eagle – a lonely male who haunts the slopes of Riggindale.

OLD MAN OF CONISTON (2,645 feet/803 metres)

West of Coniston village and its lake is the Old Man of Coniston, which you can climb from the village via Church Beck. You'll see old abandoned slate mines and spoil heap on the northeastern slopes of the mountain. From its summit you get a lovely view of Sellafield nuclear power station; even more striking, and closer at hand, is Dow Crag, which is popular with climbers.

*

Dales are valleys, sometimes dramatic, usually very pretty, and unlike mountains and fells they can be explored easily on foot, or – even more easily – by motor car, but of course you must never admit that... Here, in alphabetical order, are some of the loveliest.

BORROWDALE

Borrowdale is one of the prettiest valleys in the Lakes, but it gets very crowded. Despite what the early travellers said, it does not have jaws, but it does have spectacular views. It is the southern extension of the Vale of Derwentwater, and is easy to get to from Keswick, with a variety of contrasting scenery. A good area from which to walk, its low-lying and higher fells are easily accessible and so are many valley walks. The drive around the west side of Derwentwater provides good views of the lake.

Borrowdale seems to come to an end just beyond Grange village, where the slopes of Grange Fell and Castle Crag come together to give barely enough room for the river and road to pass through – hence the notion of jaws. Don't be put off – the valley opens up beyond and continues a long way down to the village of Seatoller and then up to Seathwaite (not to be confused with the Duddon Valley Seathwaite, to the south).

*

Just south of Grange village in Borrowdale Valley is the Bowder Stone. One of Lakeland's most famous features, this is a large, isolated rock, apparently in a state of delicate balance (it's 30 feet high, 60 feet long, and there are about 1,900 tons of it). It stands away from the rock face, overlooking the valley. How it got there, no one knows. A ladder allows you to climb to the top. It is perfectly safe, but just try walking under the overhanging sides of it – quite unnerving. There's a car park nearby and a well-marked footpath to the stone.

DUDDON VALLEY

Duddon Valley, also known as Dunnerdale, is the valley of the River Duddon in southern Lakeland. The river rises on the southern side of the Pike of Blisco and flows into the sea in a wide estuary at Duddon Sands, just north of Barrow-in-Furness. The whole valley is a delight, with plenty of car parking and pleasant walks on the surrounding fells; ideal for picnicking and swimming.

An advertisement for the Borrowdale Hotel.

DERWENTWATER LAKE.

THE BORROWDALE HOTEL,

BORROWDALE, KESWICK.

Patronized by T.R.H. the Prince of Wales and Prince Arthur,
and the Leading Nobility of Great Britain.

THE above large establishment is the *only* Hotel situated immediately at the Head of
Derwentwater at the entrance of the picturesque Vale of Borrowdale, and commands the
grandest views of Lakes, Mountains, and Valleys of this the most romantic part of the
Lake District. Parties visiting this Hotel may safely rely upon the best attendance and
all the comforts of home. An Omnibus meets all Trains at the Keswick Station. Posting
in all its branches. Mountain Ponies, experienced Guides, Boatmen, &c. Good Boating
on the Lake. Fishing Free to those staying in the Hotel.

HOT, COLD, AND SHOWER BATHS.

PARTIES BOARDED BY DAY, WEEK, OR MONTH, ON REASONABLE TERMS.

THOMAS COWARD, PROPRIETOR.

9357 BORROWDALE: THE BOWDER STONE.

At the northern end is Birks Bridge, a little packhorse bridge in a renowned beauty spot.

Wordsworth wrote thirty-four sonnets about this charming river. The last poem, 'Afterthought', contains the oft-quoted lines:

Still glides the stream; and shall forever glide. . .
The Form remains, the Function never dies. . .

The Rev. Robert Walker (1709–1802) was curate of Seathwaite in the Duddon Valley (not to be confused with the Borrowdale Seathwaite, to the north). 'Wonderful Walker' was known throughout Lakeland for his care and kindness. Despite living on a pittance all his life, he gave endlessly to the poor. Wordsworth wrote about him in his Duddon sonnets.

ENNERDALE

Ennerdale, the upper valley of the River Ehen in the western Lakes, is one of the few Lakeland valleys not properly accessible by road. It is wild and isolated and dramatic, with Steeple and Pillar (see page 102) rising above the dark conifer plantations. The road goes along the north shore of the lake as far as Bowness Point (a good viewpoint). Then you have to walk.

ESKDALE

Eskdale, in the southwestern Lakes, is very popular with tourists, though only the lower half – from Boot – is really well known to visitors. The head of the dale lies at Esk Hause in wild and dramatic scenery, while the foot is among the plains and sand dunes at Newbiggin, close to Ravenglass.

The Ravenglass and Eskdale Railway, a minimum-gauge heritage railway known locally as 'La'al Ratty', takes passengers on a forty-minute journey from Ravenglass on the coast to Dalegarth station near Boot (see also page 302).

*

A postcard of the Bowder Stone in Borrowdale.

If you find yourself in these southwest Cumbrian parts, you could always visit Muncaster Castle, just to the east of Ravenglass and overlooking the River Esk. Like many other Cumbrian stately habitations, Muncaster Castle is based on a defensive pele tower, and was built in 1325 to keep the marauding Scots at bay. In the 1860s, the fourth Lord Muncaster had it rebuilt to make a tasteful mansion. It is still lived in by the Pennington family and has been their ancestral home since the thirteenth century. It contains furniture, tapestries and paintings, including some by Joshua Reynolds and Thomas Gainsborough. The gardens are magnificent in early summer, when the rhododendrons and azaleas are at their best. Viewed against the background of the Lakeland fells, they are spectacular.

And yes, Muncaster Castle used to have one of its own unique selling points – it was the headquarters of the British Owl Trust. Now they have moved, but Muncaster still has a hawk and owl centre. It also has a vole maze.

LANGDALE

Langdale, west of Ambleside, is the most popular valley in the Lake District. It consists of two dales, joining at Elter Water and separated by Lingmoor Fell, called Great Langdale and Little Langdale. Great Langdale is the more popular and the little winding road that runs its length is sometimes crammed with cars in mid-summer. It has dramatic scenery: as you drive up the valley, the Langdale Pikes suddenly rear up in front of you.

At the head of the valley, the Old Dungeon Ghyll Hotel is a famous meeting place for climbers and walkers.

SWINDALE

Swindale, on the far eastern side of Lakeland, is reached from Bampton or Shap. It's a lovely long valley, usually forgotten by the hordes. Rolling fells provide plenty of interest with low-level and higher walks, especially onto the ridges, with good views down into the neighbouring valleys. There's no proper road up it; this is a walkers' valley.

VALE OF LORTON

The Vale of Lorton is not technically a dale, more a sequence of valleys, but it's the lushest, prettiest part of the northern Lakes. It's best to explore it from Cockermouth to get the full shape and extent. Coming from Keswick, you can get into it over the Whinlatter Pass, hitting the village of Lorton, where you turn left and follow the River Cocker upstream and, very gently and subtly, three marvellous lakes carefully unfold themselves for your inspection.

First there's Loweswater, then the bigger Crummock Water and finally, the most popular of the three, Buttermere. Go right to the end of the valley and you can get back towards Keswick, over Honister Pass this time. There are excellent walks, with some nice hamlets and pubs to explore along the way.

WASDALE

Wasdale is the most inaccessible valley in the western Lakes, and therefore one of the quietest, even at the height of the season. Much of the valley floor is occupied by Wastwater (see pages 65–8).

*

Lakeland has several dramatic mountain passes suitable for motor traffic. Some are famous. Two are notorious. All of them are exciting for those lazy motorists who never leave the wheel, but like to boast that they have scaled the Lakeland heights... Here they are, starting with the Big Two and ending with the highest of the lot.

HARDKNOTT PASS (1,291 feet/394 metres)

Hardknott Pass is the Lake District's most exciting road, hair-raising in places, with one-in-three gradients, sharp bends and a delightful sheer drop on the west-hand side. It can also get very busy in summer, with numerous hold-ups as motorists shuffle about on the steep bits to get past each other. Just below the summit, on the Eskdale side, there are parking places.

Near the top of the pass, on the left as you go up from Eskdale, is Hardknott Fort, which should not be missed. You *can* easily miss it from the road. There's not a lot to see compared with a Roman site like Birdoswald on Hadrian's Wall, but it's a dramatic site guarding the road from Galava (see Ambleside on page 132) to Glannaventa (Ravenglass). The parade ground is fascinating and the views fantastic. The Roman name was Mediobogdum and the walls still stand, though not very high.

You get a wonderful idea of why the Romans eventually came to a grinding halt in these far-flung places. Visitors often stand and think, poor sods, coming all the way from sunny Rome and ending up stuck here – but of course the vast majority of those serving in Britain were recruits from countries already conquered in Eastern and Northern Europe, well used to the cold back home.

WRYNOSE PASS (1,281 feet/391 metres)
Wrynose Pass is the second of the Big Two and probably the more famous, though staff at tourist information centres frequently get asked the way to Rhino Pass or even Buffalo Pass. Linking Little Langdale with the head of the Duddon Valley (see page 104), Wrynose is notoriously steep and narrow (although the best is yet to come). There are places where it is impossible for two cars to pass, so special passing places are provided. These are not laybys and anyone parking in them deserves to have their handbrake released. At the summit is a pillar of rock called Three Shires Stone, which used to mark the meeting point of the boundaries of Lancashire, Westmorland and Cumberland. It is a place where traditionalists still shed a few tears.

HONISTER PASS (1,176 feet/359 metres)
Honister Pass links Seatoller in Borrowdale with the southern end of Buttermere. There are one-in-four gradients in places and on the Buttermere side it can get narrow. It's not a brilliant route for scenery. At the top is a green-slate quarry. Not a difficult pass.

An old advertisement for tours with Cumberland Motor Services.

CUMBERLAND MOTOR SERVICES LTD.

GRAND
COACHING AND WALKING COMBINATION
The Finest in the Lake District.

....

OVER
HONISTER & WHINLATTER
PASSES

By COACH alongside beautiful Derwentwater, through the Rocky Jaws of Borrowdale and the old world village of Rosthwaite to Seatoller.

WALK from Seatoller over the Honister Pass to Buttermere. 5½ miles.

Rejoining COACH at Buttermere, "The Secret Valley," along the shores of Crummock Water, passing through Lorton Valley, then over the Whinlatter Pass, viewing Bassenthwaite Lake and the Skiddaw range in all its grandeur, thence via Braithwaite and Portinscale to Keswick.

Daily Operation — Sundays included — until 27th September.

DEPART	ARRIVE
Keswick (Bus Station)	**Seatoller**
9-20, 11-10 a.m., 1-50 p.m.	10-0, 11-50 a.m., 2-30 p.m.

Walking Distance over Honister Pass to Buttermere, 5½ miles.

DEPART		ARRIVE
Buttermere (Victoria Hotel)	via Whinlatter Pass	**Keswick** (Bus Station)
5-30 p.m.		6-30 p.m.

FARE (Single).
Keswick to Seatoller, 1/3 — Buttermere to Keswick, 2/2.

For other Services to and from Borrowdale & Seatoller, see Official Time Table.

FURTHER INFORMATION Apply :—BUS STATION, KESWICK.

T. MEAGEEN, Managing Director.

James Usher, Printer, Main Street, Keswick.

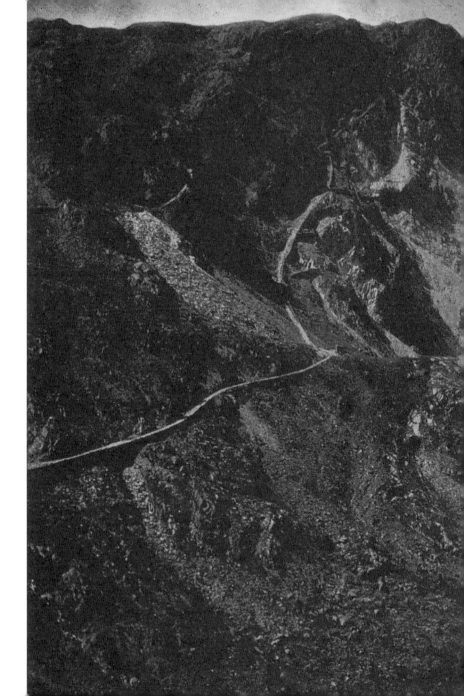

Honister Pass.

NEWLANDS PASS (1,100 feet/335 metres)

Newlands Pass is the most direct route from Keswick over to Buttermere village. It starts off yummy and easy-looking, through Beatrix Potter-type countryside, but gets steep and wild on the top.

WHINLATTER PASS (1,043 feet/318 metres)

Whinlatter Pass goes from Braithwaite, near Keswick, to High Lorton. It's the easiest of all the passes, although there are occasional steep sections. Going up from the Keswick end, there are good views over Bassenthwaite, with parking places. A lot of the view is obscured, however, as you enter the Forestry Commission's Thornthwaite Forest.

KIRKSTONE PASS (1,489 feet/454 metres)

Kirkstone Pass connects Windermere and Ambleside with Ullswater. This is the pass that all the TV crews rush to when snow begins and they want to show everyone that the Lake District is snowed in.

From Windermere, the road is good, with a long, interesting descent to Patterdale. To get to the pass from Ambleside, you go up a very narrow, steep road, aptly called The Struggle (it is almost opposite the Bridge House). Nineteenth-century travellers used to have to leave their coaches and walk alongside the horses up this part. It's not quite as bad as that today, but there are some sharp bends to trap the unwary. The Kirkstone Pass Inn is the third-highest pub in England.

*

Most Lakeland becks or streams, as they come down those there fells and mountains, have a tumbling force of water or waterfall of some kind along the way. Many of them are small, hidden and unsung. Some reveal their presence by doing their own gentle singing: *gurgle gurgle, trickle trickle, tra la.* Don't expect to see them at their best after a long, dry spell, or even to be able to find them.

Oh yes, tropical days often do happen in a Lakeland summer. After a heavy rainfall, that's when they are at their most noisy, powerful and pounding.

TAYLOR GILL FORCE

Taylor Gill Force is above Borrowdale, at Stockley Bridge. This is what the experts generally consider to be Lakeland's finest waterfall. A spectacular setting with an ambling mountain stream, which transforms itself into a 140-foot cascade. It can be seen from below the bridge, but for the best views follow the path to the right of the falls.

SCALE FORCE

Scale Force is the Lake District's longest waterfall, at 172 feet. The path to the falls goes from Buttermere village and the falls themselves are hidden in a narrow, tree-lined gorge. More for the real waterfall collector than the average visitor.

AIRA FORCE

Aira Force is probably the most famous of the Lake District's falls, possibly because of its emotive name, which flows off the tongue. Why did those two daring pilots, Leeming and Hinkler, not land here instead of Helvellyn (see page 91)?

It is on the west side of Ullswater (see page 53), near Dockray, just a few minutes' pleasant walk from the public car park. The main force falls 70 feet from below a stone footbridge. You also get a good viewpoint from the path, which ends just below the falls. If the sun is shining, look out for the rainbow.

STOCK GHYLL FORCE

Stock Ghyll Force is on the fellside behind Ambleside (see page 132). This delightful little waterfall is easily reached by walking from the town centre up the road that runs behind the Salutation Hotel. A nice wooded walk to a 70-foot cascade flowing under a stone footbridge. Not spectacular, but very pretty.

LAKELAND

LODORE FALLS

Lodore Falls is at the southern end of Derwentwater and is easily reached from the road, but perhaps the nicest way to view it is on a boat, sitting down on the lake. This 40-foot cataract is in a chasm surrounded by woods and crags. You have to pay to see it and there is an honesty box, which must be unique for a natural feature of this kind.

Robert Southey wrote a children's poem about the Lodore Falls, 'The Cataract of Lodore' (c. 1823), which was memorised and chanted aloud by millions of Victorian school pupils. The poet answers a little boy's question of 'How does the water / Come down at Lodore?' It does go on rather, but here is a bit of it...

> Retreating and beating and meeting and sheeting,
> Delaying and straying and playing and spraying,
> Advancing and prancing and glancing and dancing,
> Recoiling, turmoiling and toiling and boiling,
> And gleaming and streaming and steaming and beaming,
> And rushing and flushing and brushing and gushing,
> And flapping and rapping and clapping and slapping,
> And curling and whirling and purling and twirling,
> And thumping and plumping and bumping and jumping,
> And dashing and flashing and splashing and clashing;
> And so never ending, but always descending,
> Sounds and motions for ever and ever are blending
> All at once and all o'er, with a mighty uproar, -
> And this way the water comes down at Lodore.

A VIEW ABOUT VIEWS

I have ten different Lakeland collections, i.e. collections of stuff somehow connected with the Lake District and Cumbria. They include Wainwright books and drawings, Beatrix Potter books, Carlisle United programmes, letters

Stock Ghyll Force.

from famous residents, posters and advertisements, guidebooks, Carr's biscuits memorabilia and prewar Lakeland hotel letterheads.

But perhaps my biggest collection in terms of units is my collection of Lakeland postcards. I probably have about 1,000 of them.

Guess which postcards are seen as the most boring, and are the least loved by collectors of Lakeland postcards? Here's a clue: in terms of prices, the cheapest cards are the ones showing famous Lakeland scenes – Ullswater at dusk, a peaceful morning on Windermere, Scafell from Borrowdale and so on. You can buy these sorts of cards for 50p or even find them at the 10p bargain box at postcard fairs. Yet these are the shots that Lakeland is famous for, which have been photographed millions of times and rhapsodised about in poetry and prose, and have drawn millions of tourists over the last 250 years. So why are postcards of Lakeland views so unloved and unregarded?

Partly it's because a postcard is pretty titchy, just six inches by four: how can you do justice to an awesome natural wonder on such a tiny canvas? Another reason is that in the early twentieth century the postcard producers tried to colour the cards, with results that were horrible, lurid and unreal.

But the real reason why postcards of Lakeland views are unloved by postcard connoisseurs is that postcards of Lakeland views *are* boring. They always depict the same old, same old corny Lakeland views. A postcard of Skiddaw and Derwentwater in 2016 is pretty much the same as a postcard of Skiddaw and Derwentwater in 1926. Only the printing and typography gives away the different dates.

The Lakeland postcards that are considered desirable by collectors like me and cost real money are the ones not showing views but showing buildings, cars and people. Postcards of the Moot Hall and main street in Keswick in the 1930s can keep me fascinated, noting the changes in the shops, the clothes, the vehicles.

While I will dismiss yet another shot of Windermere looking up the lake, I will always buy a shot of, say, the Old England Hotel, with people sitting out in the garden in their best frocks having tea, looking at the lake.

The best view I know of Derwentwater is that famous painting of the couple having tea in the dining room in a hotel under Skiddaw, looking through the window towards the lake.

Two hundred years ago, the early tourist guides would list their most picturesque views, which they called stations, telling you where to stand and how to look. I have often wondered what would be considered the best views today by a visiting writer of experience and discernment, telling us what to look out for.

Sir Simon Jenkins was brave enough recently to produce a book called *England's 100 Best Views*. He is a friend I used to work with. He still works as a journalist and has written many books. He has also been on several worthy national committees and been chairman of the National Trust. He does have awfully good taste.

I was pleased to see that eleven of his Best Views were in Cumbria – as opposed to only six for the whole of the Northeast, ha ha, and just six for London. The Lakeland views are: Borrowdale, Buttermere, Castlerigg, Derwentwater, Gummer's How, Langdale, Ullswater, Wasdale Head, Wrynose and Hardknott, Hartside Pass and High Cup Nick. I have to admit I didn't know the last one. (It's in the village of Dufton, looking down into the Eden Valley.)

They are stunning landscapes, all beautiful, but they are devoid of people and things. Admittedly people and things are not Sir Simon's objective in *England's 100 Best Views* – he has done other books about houses and churches. Surely the thing about a good view is that you want to actually *be* there, enjoy it in the flesh, take it in three-dimensionally – in your eyes, your body, your soul. On the page, and even more so on a postcard, it can easily get diminished.

So what's my fave Lakeland view? I have two – both from inside our house at Loweswater. From my room I love looking out at Grasmoor, especially when the sun sets. Going upstairs and entering my wife's room, which I am not supposed to do without knocking, I am always surprised by joy when I catch a glimpse of Mellbreak, perfectly framed through her window.

4

Lakeland Towns and Villages
and What to See There

The full perfection of Keswick consists of three
circumstances, beauty, horror and immensity united.

JOHN BROWN, 1767

ONE OF THE JOYS OF LAKELAND, AMONG ITS MANY attractions and advantages, is that it is not urban. You don't rush to Lakeland to walk around towns and streets and suburbs and estates. But they do exist. And there is also still some industry, such as quarries, paper mills and a few little factories, lurking inside the National Park. At one time, there was a fair bit of industry in Lakeland – mainly mines and quarries. The discovery of lead in the Borrowdale Valley in the 1500s led to the start of the Cumberland pencil industry, which continues to this day.

The county of Cumbria even has one city, the border city of Carlisle, and as I write it is the only Cumbrian town with a football team in the Football League. (There used to be three; alongside Carlisle, Barrow and Workington both had long spells in the Football League, mainly in League Three, Division North.) Carlisle is the county capital, but it is outside the National Park, as are Barrow and Workington. Inside the National Park boundaries, which stretch all the way to the West Coast, it is more or less rural – though in Keswick on a bank holiday you might well think you had landed in Oxford Street.

One strange feature of the National Park boundary is that it makes what appear to be spiteful detours to exclude two towns: Kendal in the south and Cockermouth in the north, both of which are always assumed and accepted by locals and visitors to be true Lakeland towns in their history, economy, architecture and character.

Kendal, for example, while not in the National Park, is where the National Park offices are located. This presumably must be a huge asset. They don't really have to apply to themselves when they want to put in a new lavatory window or garage, or have roof slates the colour and texture they fancy – things which, inside the National Park, the National Park planning people can be awfully sticky about.

Lakeland Hotspots

The towns and villages that are honoured and pleased to be proper Lakeland towns (i.e. inside the National Park boundaries), such as Windermere, Keswick, Ambleside and Grasmere, do tend to become horribly busy in the holiday seasons, being overrun with visitors wandering six abreast in their shorts and boots and anoraks, going up and down the main streets looking for places where they can buy more shorts and boots and anoraks, plus chips. Fortunately almost every shop is able to supply these vital needs. Last year in Keswick I counted fifty-three shops where you can buy outdoor clothes.

BOWNESS AND WINDERMERE (population 8,500)

The largest town inside the National Park. And it can certainly seem like it in the summer holidays when it becomes the number-one tourist attraction of the Lake District – especially for day-trippers. Windermere is the only central Lakeland town to have its own railway station. It has the feeling of a seaside resort, rather than an inland town, with most of the usual seaside amenities, but it manages, if only just, to avoid the worst of seaside squalor, like amusement arcades, for example. It tries hard to remain dignified, despite the hordes. Technically, Bowness-on-Windermere and Windermere are two towns, but they are virtually joined together, always considered as one, and usually just referred to as Windermere.

The Bowness part is right on the lakeside, an ancient village in its own right, centred round the fifteenth-century St Martin's Church. (Martin was a Roman officer who divided his cloak in half to help a beggar. Jolly kind of him.) The name Bowness comes from Bulness, meaning a promontory that looks like a bull's head, and it does, if you study the map, jutting out into the lake beside Bowness Bay.

Windermere was originally a little village called Birthwaite, about a mile away inland. It only became known as Windermere after the arrival of the railway in 1848. As the station was called Windermere, and Windermere –

Bowness Bay.

Boat Landings.

The Wrench Series, No. 2917.

meaning the lake – was what they wanted to see, the Lancashire hordes referred to everything around it as Windermere.

When Wordsworth predicted that the little village would be inundated by 'the Advance of the Ten Thousand', he turned out to be right. Bowness and Windermere were transformed almost overnight. And not just by the hordes who came for day trips, but also by the new wealthy from Lancashire who built splendid mansions, many of them Italianate or Gothic fantasies – grand holiday homes to show off their own grandness. There still is a lot of money around Windermere, and quite a few palatial homes and private yacht harbours, but many of the bigger Victorian mansions are no longer private homes.

Brockhole, the National Park Centre, used to be one of them, and so was Belsfield, which is now a hotel. Belsfield was built by H. W. Schneider (see page 258), a tycoon who used to commute each day to his industrial empire in Barrow, travelling in his own launch down Windermere to Lakeside, then by a special carriage on the Furness Railway to Barrow. Ah, those were the days.

As befits the Lake District's biggest town, there are plenty of tourist amenities here: lake steamers, a regular ferry across the lake from Bowness, a bus station, masses of hotels and guesthouses, shops, boats, Windermere Steamboat Museum, a cinema, the Old Laundry Theatre, The World of Beatrix Potter and lots of restaurants, not all of them selling chips. It is handy for Beatrix Potter country, just a short ferry journey across the lake, and also for the National Park Centre at Brockhole, along the lakeside road towards Ambleside to the north.

The view of the lake from Orrest Head, a hill just north of the town of Windermere, is excellent, and it's a doddle to climb. On a very clear day you might even glimpse Morecambe Bay and Blackpool Tower. But oh, those summertime crowds.

Bowness in an old postcard.

KESWICK (population 4,762)

'The full perfection of Keswick consists of three circumstances, beauty, horror and immensity united.' So observed John Brown in *A Description of the Lake at Keswick*, published in 1767. 'Of beauty it hath little, nature having left it almost a desert; neither its small extent nor the diminutive and lifeless forms of the hills admit magnificence.'

Goodness, he was in a bad mood. It couldn't have been all the cagoules that upset him, not in 1767. Perhaps it was the miners, coming back from the lead mines, desperate to get to the pubs. Later guidebooks and writers have generally raved about Keswick, though some have been a bit snotty about Derwentwater, comparing it unfavourably with Ullswater.

Nonetheless, Keswick has always been pretty pleased with itself and enjoys being regally referred to as 'The Queen of Lakeland'. It does, in fact, have a fantastic setting, sandwiched between Derwentwater and Borrowdale on one side and the guardians of Skiddaw and Blencathra looking out over it from the other. The best view of the town, and the lake beyond, is seen from the lower slopes of Skiddaw, around Underscar.

But because it is a tighter, more closed-in little town than Windermere, and immensely popular, and gets the real climbers and hairy-legged walkers as well as the day-trippers, it always feels more crowded on busy weekends. Apart from outdoor shops, it is also said to have more bed and breakfasts and guesthouses per head of population than anywhere else in the country.

The lakeshore walk, along Lake Road, houses the first-class Theatre by the Lake. The oldest building is Crosthwaite Church at the northwest corner of the town. The church's foundations date from 1181, but most of the fabric of the building dates from the fourteenth century and later. Southey is buried in the churchyard, as is Canon Rawnsley, co-founder of the National Trust (see pages 224–9). Brandelhow Park, on the southwestern shore of Derwentwater, was the first property to be acquired by the Trust in 1902.

Keswick became prosperous with the arrival of the mining industry in the sixteenth century. Mining engineers were imported from Germany to look for copper, lead, silver and iron. They were treated with suspicion by the locals and forced to make their homes on Derwent Island, but they must have overcome the hostility as German surnames can still be found among the local population. The town became famous for the black lead mined in Borrowdale and so the Cumberland Pencil Company was born. Close to the Cumberland Pencil Museum on Main Street (see page 129) is Greta Hall, a fine Georgian house where Coleridge and Southey lived (see pages 199 and 201). Greta Hall is now a family home that offers posh B&B services.

A handy guide to Keswick and its transport links from 1898.

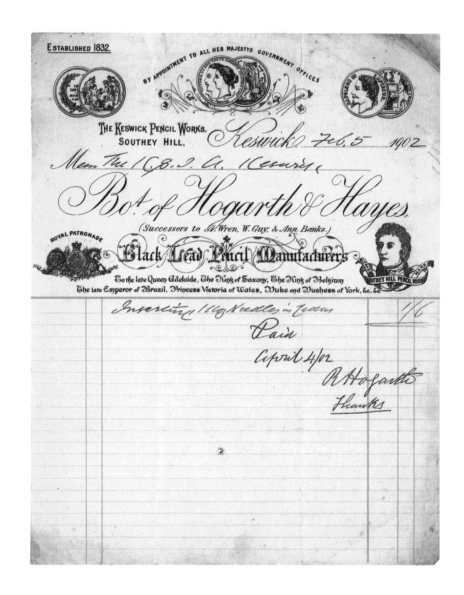

Overlooking the town is Windebrowe, where William and Dorothy Wordsworth lived for a short time before moving to Dove Cottage.

In 1865 the Cockermouth–Penrith railway line opened and put Keswick on the mass-tourist map. But, unlike at Windermere, the railway at Keswick has gone, though the old railway line makes an excellent walk.

Most of the buildings in the centre of Keswick are Victorian, though the Moot Hall, in the market square, was built in 1813 (on the site of a sixteenth-century building). Look out for the unusual one-handed clock on the tower at the northern end of the hall. One visitor described Moot Hall as a cross between an art gallery and a public lavatory, but it actually contains a tourist information centre.

*

The Cumberland Pencil Museum is in the northwest part of Keswick, beside the river, about a ten-minute walk from the centre of town. It is a good museum for children – and fantastic if you happen to be a pencil freak. It has been billed as 'the story of the pencil brought to life', and lately 'home of the world's first pencils'. They have pencil-making machines, a video display about pencils, drawing competitions and a busy shop.

Don't miss the very clever Wartime Pencils, which have a secret compartment, containing a compass and a map of Germany. The museum also boasts the World's Longest Pencil (it's in the *Guinness Book of Records*) – 26 feet long. Nowadays it's a celebrity and often out and about, raising money for charity. So if you particularly want to see it, ring in advance to make sure it's in residence.

*

Keswick Museum and Art Gallery is one of Cumbria's oddest museums, more an idiosyncratic collection of strange objects than a normal municipal museum

An invoice – dating from 1902 – from the Keswick Pencil Works.

– a direct descendant of the odd museum that Peter Crosthwaite had in eighteenth-century Keswick (see pages 126–32). It has some good literary items – letters and documents relating to Wordsworth, Southey, Coleridge and Walpole. Look out, also, for an original copy of *The Three Bears*, which Southey wrote. (In his original version it's an old woman who eats their porridge – Goldilocks is a later addition.)

For decades, the best-known and best-loved items here have been a set of nineteenth-century musical stones and a box marked '500-year-old cat'. The stones are ordinary stones, laid out like a xylophone, which you can play, as they are hard to damage, and get a tune. They were played before Queen Victoria in 1848. Apparently she was amused.

When I visited the museum and opened the 500-year-old-cat box, ready to scoff at the mangy skeleton inside, there was this ghastly, ghostly, loud creaking sound of ancient hinges being forced apart. Then I realised it was a tape, secreted somewhere inside, which plays once you open the lid. Little boys and little girls, and old boys and old girls, love it. Some modern tricks do help old museums. . .

✳

East of Keswick, and just a thirty-minute walk from the town, is Castlerigg Stone Circle. It has a fantastic setting, surrounded by high fells (you can see some of the highest peaks in Lakeland from here, including Helvellyn, Skiddaw, Grasmoor and Blencathra), though the stones themselves are not all that impressive; there are thirty-eight of them in a circle, roughly 90 feet across. The circle is about 3,000 to 4,000 years old. Like the economy, no one can explain it.

If you fancy yet more stones, three miles from Keswick in the direction of Penrith is the Threlkeld Quarry and Mining Museum. It's quite hard to find, so watch out carefully for the notices. Don't head for Threlkeld village – it's on the other side of the A66. It's a huge site, some seventy acres, in and

Keswick Market Place in an old postcard.

Market Place, Keswick.

around an old quarry, with a great deal to see, including old locomotives, mining artefacts and minerals.

On the site itself, you can go underground on guided trips, inspect the old quarry buildings and vintage machinery, and enter the loco shed, where a loco might be on the track. Mining played a vital part in Cumbria's history, so it's good that these sorts of mining museums manage to struggle on, relying heavily on volunteers, reminding us of how the landscape used to look.

AMBLESIDE (population 2,671)

Beautifully situated in the Rothay Valley, one mile north of the head of Lake Windermere and roughly in the middle of Lakeland, Ambleside is one of the major centres for the climbing and walking fraternity. But it is also a good jumping-off point for the general visitor, and has more escape routes to the surrounding fells and lakes than anywhere else in the Lake District. Like Windermere and Keswick, it gets chocka in summer, but unlike some other places (e.g. Grasmere), it doesn't die in winter and can still be quite lively and interesting when the winter fell-walking enthusiasts start arriving. The town's name comes from the Old Norse words for summer pasture by a river.

Ambleside has a long history, owing to its position at the crossing of many old pack-horse routes. The Romans had a fort at Waterhead, called Galava, one mile south of the town. Probably built around AD 79, it protected the road that ran from Brougham over Hardknott to Ravenglass. Few stones from the fort remain, but the layout is still visible from the surrounding fells – especially from Todd Crag on Loughrigg Fell to the northeast. The field in which it stands is owned by the National Trust. The local name for it is Borrans Fort.

The town's best-known building, or at least the most photographed, is the tiny Bridge House. It's not much to boast about, really, as it is just one up and one down, but it happens to be an actual little bridge, over a little stream, Stock Ghyll, in Rydal Road. Local legend says that it was built by a Scotsman to avoid paying land tax, but it was in fact the apple-storing house belonging to Ambleside Hall, when this part of the town was covered with orchards. It has also been a weaver's shop, a family home, a cobbler's and a tea shop. It is now owned by the National Trust.

The oldest part of Ambleside dates from the fifteenth century and is on the Kirkstone side of the River Rothay. This was once a centre for corn and bobbin mills, and restored waterwheels can be seen just below the bridge on North Road and next to the National Trust's Bridge House.

Originally, the railway was meant to come right through to Ambleside from Windermere, which was what Wordsworth was so bothered about (see pages 31–2). (There were plans to carry it on up to Keswick and put a tunnel through Dunmail Raise). But the plan was shelved and nineteenth-century tourists had to come up from Windermere by steam launch and charabanc.

The large building near the centre of town used to be a teacher-training college named after its founder, the educationist Charlotte Mason, one of Ambleside's famous residents. Others have included Harriet Martineau, Dr Arnold of Rugby and the Liberal statesman W. E. Forster. One of Ambleside's more intriguing twentieth-century residents was the Dadaist artist and poet Kurt Schwitters, famous for his collages, who settled here in 1942 having fled Nazi persecution. You can see some of Schwitters's work in the excellent Armitt Museum and Gallery, which is well worth a visit (see page 135).

There's also a lovely walk beside Stock Ghyll to a spectacular 70-foot waterfall much loved by the Victorians (the walk starts behind the Salutation Hotel; see also page 115). Of course you're also handily placed here for a visit to Wordsworth's house at Rydal Mount (see page 192). And don't forget the Windermere steamers and launches, and all those rowing boats for hire. . .

*

In 1912 three Brontë-type sisters – Marie Louisa, Annie Maria and Sophia Armitt – who devoted themselves to writing and the arts, founded a library in Ambleside as a scholarly resource for the local community. The library was

HOLD BRIDGE HOUSE, AMBLESIDE.
ABRAHAMS SERIES.

subsequently supported by the great and the good of the times, including Canon Rawnsley, Beatrix Potter, Arthur Ransome and G. M. Trevelyan.

The Armitt is now a proper museum and not just a library (as it was for many years), and is open to the public in a very classy new building (though it took a bit of a beating from Storm Desmond in December 2015).

The Armitt Museum and Gallery now houses the largest collection of fungi watercolours done by Beatrix Potter (that was an early passion of hers, before she wrote *Peter Rabbit*), early Lakeland photographs, rare books of literary and Cumbrian interest, archaeological relics and literary manuscripts. They also have paintings by Kurt Schwitters and collections devoted to John Ruskin and Harriet Martineau.

The best stuff here is the Beatrix Potter collection, downstairs in the museum, for which there is an admission charge. Ask nicely and they might let you put on white gloves and look at a first edition of *Peter Rabbit*. The library is upstairs, with 27,000 priceless books and maps, and is free.

✳

Rydal Hall, on the outskirts of Rydal village, north of Ambleside, is not to be confused with the nearby Rydal Mount (see page 192), the home of Wordsworth. The hall itself is mainly Georgian (though parts go back to before 1600) and is owned by the Diocese of Carlisle. Now used for conferences, holidays and retreats, the hall itself is not open to the public, but it stands in thirty acres of grounds and the formal gardens have been opened up. The gardens, like those at Brockhole (see page 50), were originally laid out by Thomas Mawson.

The opening up of the gardens means that the public can once again visit the famous Lower Falls, much painted by the early tourists. Nearby is the grotto, a summerhouse once regularly visited by Wordsworth. The gardens also have a nice fountain and splendid views over Rydal to Lake Windermere.

A postcard of the Old Bridge House in Ambleside.

GRASMERE (population 841)

Grasmere is everyone's idea of a picturesque Lakeland village and is forever associated with William and Dorothy Wordsworth. Grasmere does look very pretty, especially if seen from the path known as Loughrigg Terrace, just to the south, looking down over the lake with the village against the background of Helm Crag and Dunmail Raise, but the surrounding fells can give it a damp, claustrophobic air, especially in winter.

The village is almost wholly orientated towards tourists, and is full of cafés and shops. In winter it used to die completely, though the presence of knitwear shops now encourages the village to stay open out of season. In the summer, it is overrun – the sports field becomes an unsightly mass of caravans and the roads into the village become blocked with coaches disgorging hordes of tourists in search of Dove Cottage. For all this, Grasmere thinks rather a lot of itself, disdaining what it sees as the commercialism of Dove Cottage and the Wordsworth Museum while continuing to feed off the visitors they bring to the area.

A member of the Grasmere Women's Institute once compiled a short history of the village, which contained the following notable sentence on the subject of 'off-comers': 'Grasmere is the poorer for the losses it has sustained during the last twenty-five years, losses of people who are not matched by the newer people who have come into the village, many of whom may be good and nice people but are not of the same caliber as their predecessors.' So, please don't spit or swear, especially near a resident.

The village itself is really a string of hamlets along the old pack-horse route to Whitehaven. The road used to come over White Moss and past Dove Cottage, in the days when it was an inn.

The present main road was built in the 1830s. Coming from Ambleside you encounter a rather nasty bend, just before coming into view of the lake; this is known locally as Penny Rock, because blasting the rocks to put the road through added a penny to the rates. There is a corpse track over White Moss from Rydal. Coffins were once carried along here to Grasmere Church.

Up the hill, past Dove Cottage, there is a large, flat stone known as a 'coffin stone', where the bearers used to rest.

Most of the village buildings are nineteenth or early twentieth century, though the surrounding farms are far older. Grasmere Church, dedicated to St Oswald, dates from the thirteenth century and is the scene of one of Lakeland's rush-bearing ceremonies (see pages 307–9). The Wordsworth family graves are in the churchyard. Grasmere Sports Day is one of the oldest and most popular traditional events in the Lake District (probably dating back to Viking times) and involves people from all over the North. At one time, even Dove Cottage would close down on Sports Day so that the staff could go along. Now they have to keep at it, catering for the hordes.

CONISTON (population 868)

Probably the most disappointing of the better-known Lakeland villages. Coniston has a magnificent setting, but the grey, stone-built village has little character of its own and is almost wholly given over to the tourist industry. Its best feature is the way the Old Man of Coniston (see page 103) rises dramatically behind the houses when seen from the village centre. The road from the south can be rather dreary, apart from Blawith Common. Still, Coniston remains a good centre for walkers, though climbers now seem to prefer the Langdales and Borrowdale.

Coniston grew up in the eighteenth century as a mining village, though copper was mined locally as far back as Norman times. In the sixteenth century, Keswick's resident German miners were brought in and the ore extracted was sent up to Keswick for smelting. The area around Church Beck is still referred to as Coppermines Valley.

Coniston was once served by a railway line that came up from Furness. The closure of the line rendered the village rather inaccessible compared to the central Lakeland villages. The area's most famous resident was John Ruskin, who acquired Brantwood on the eastern shores of Coniston Water in 1871 (see page 220); the sixteenth-century St Andrew's Church in the centre of

Coniston, showing Old Man

Coniston village contains his tomb. On the village green, just opposite the car park, a large green-slate seat acts as a memorial to Donald Campbell, who died attempting the world water speed record on the lake in 1967 (see page 58).

The name Coniston means 'the king's farm'. Coniston's oldest building is Coniston Old Hall, a sixteenth-century building just south of the village and once associated with the area's largest landowners, the Flemings. It is now owned by the National Trust and has been restored to its seventeenth-century condition.

HAWKSHEAD (population 530)

Just north of Esthwaite Water, Hawkshead is another small village with large pretensions. Hawkshead feels like a proper town, nonetheless, with its little squares and bits hidden away. It is generally reckoned to be the quaintest and prettiest village in the Lake District, and consequently it gets very crowded in mid-summer. Cars are banned from the village itself, which is a good idea, but it tends to give the village the feel of an open-air museum. It has an attractive muddle of squares and cobbled streets, overhung by timber-framed seventeenth-century buildings. It isn't too difficult to imagine what it must have been like when Wordsworth went to school here.

Hawkshead was an important wool town in the Middle Ages, hence all the handsome houses. It once had as many as seven inns. St Michael's Church, up on the hill overlooking the village, is one of the most interesting Lakeland churches. There has been a chapel or church on this site since the twelfth century, but the present building dates from about the fifteenth. Inside are decorations and painted texts dating from around 1680.

Ann Tyson's cottage is in the centre of the village, in Vicarage Lane. It is identified by a plaque, but when William Wordsworth lodged with her, Ann Tyson lived at Colthouse, just outside the village.

In 1548, William Sawrey, the vicar of Urswick, stayed at what is now the Old Courthouse. Local records say that he was besieged for two days by a

A postcard of Coniston with the Old Man looming behind the village.

'tumult of insurrection' – men armed to the teeth with swords, clubs and daggers. They demanded that he should come out, 'for they would have one of his arms or legs before going away'. Eventually, they were dispersed by neighbours. Why, or what it was all about, no one knows. The name of the village comes from Old Norse and means 'Haukr's summer pasture'.

Hawkshead can be reached via the Windermere ferry, which is handy if you are in a hurry. Apart from the sixteenth-century Grammar School (which closed in 1909 and is now a museum where you can see Wordsworth's initials carved into a desk), there is the Beatrix Potter Gallery, located in what were once the offices of her husband, William Heelis, a local solicitor.

Cumbrian Towns

Now for some of the towns that are not technically within Lakeland as defined by the boundaries of the National Park, but which hover near or on its fringes. Some of these places, like Carlisle, Penrith and Kendal (each of which claims to be 'The Gateway to the Lakes'), you might not be able to avoid if you come to Lakeland on either the mainline railway or the M6 motorway. But if the weather is too appalling, you might find that you actually *want* to visit these towns – to poke about, see some street life and historic sights, or simply to find a decent class of shop. Here they are, in alphabetical order.

CARLISLE (population 100,000)
The population figure makes it look bigger than it is – partly because they now count all the little nearby villages – but in Cumbrian terms it is a metropolis. Carlisle is Cumbria's capital city, the home of the County Council, Radio Cumbria, local television, Cumbria's only Football League team and the home of Carr's of Carlisle, the world's first biscuit factory. Not a huge place by London or even Lancashire standards, but it makes up for it with an exciting and confusing one-way system.

Carlisle in an old engraving, seen from the River Eden.

The city has a long history, much of it reflected in the architecture. It has an ancient castle and Cumbria's only cathedral, where Sir Walter Scott got married. It became an administrative centre during the Roman invasion, with much of its subsequent history revolving around its proximity to the Anglo-Scottish border (which was not always north of the city – there were times when Carlisle itself was part of Scotland). The Romans called it Luguvalium and placed a fort at Stanwix, on Hadrian's Wall, which ran along the northern outskirts of the city.

There has been a castle at Carlisle since 1092 (the first was probably built of wood), occupying a good strategic position. Throughout the Middle Ages it was continually plundered, attacked and generally demolished by marauding Scots. The castle became more and more important, and walls were built around the city. In 1568, Mary Queen of Scots fled her own country and was imprisoned in the castle. She looked out from her cell and saw people playing football, twenty a side – one of the earliest records of people playing football. Bonnie Prince Charlie and his Jacobite army seized the castle in 1745 on their way south to take over London (so they hoped), but gave up at Derby.

Carlisle Castle looks like a real castle, dark and grim, not like your soft and fancy turreted Southern castles. In the prison rooms you will find graffiti from the poor sods who were locked up many centuries ago. Today the castle houses the Border Regiment Museum.

Tullie House Museum (see below) is Carlisle's cultural *pièce de résistance*, and there's a fascinating town trail and a neat cathedral (see below). Carlisle has its own leisure centre at the Sands, and there's a good shopping precinct in The Lanes – flashy yet tasteful. There is also an excellent covered market, dating back to Victorian times, and the medieval Guildhall Museum (in a beautifully restored timber-framed building dating from 1405). The best bits are around the Old Town Hall, a little gem in pink brick, plus Fisher Street and Castle Street, now mainly pedestrianised. Hurrah.

*

The Tullie House Museum and Art Gallery is Carlisle's award-winning cultural wonderland, thanks to its massive £5 million redevelopment. The underground Millennium Gallery was added in 2002. You can actually see where the money has gone (which is not always the case when they tart up something old) and sense the care and imagination that has been lavished on all the exhibits. It's good on the Romans, the Roman Wall, the Border Reivers, Lakeland wildlife, Carr's biscuit works, the State Management brewery and local railway history. The Tullie House Museum manages to be fun yet smart and informative. It's well laid out, for young and old, and worth two hours of anyone's time.

In the art gallery shows change all the time, but the best things are the Pre-Raphaelite paintings. Carlisle has works by Edward Burne-Jones, John Everett Millais, Camille Pissarro, James Abbott McNeill Whistler, Augustus John, Paul Nash, Stanley Spencer – amazing, really, for a small provincial city. (They got them cheap in the 1930s when Sir William Rothenstein became their London art advisor.)

Before leaving, go outside and examine the original Tullie House, Carlisle's only remaining Jacobean building. The ornate lead drainpipes are works of art in themselves.

*

Carlisle Cathedral, Cumbria's only cathedral, began as an Augustinian church in the early twelfth century and was promoted to cathedral in 1133 – the only Augustinian house in England to achieve this. It's rather small, as cathedrals go, but it has a magnificent east window, one of the best in England. The west end and transepts are the earliest parts. Most of the decorated features were rebuilt following a great fire in 1292.

The Civil War took its toll on the structure and it had to wait for Victorian times for a decent restoration. Don't miss the fifteenth-century paintings behind the choir stalls and the Treasury exhibition in the superb

OVERLEAF
A postcard of the Scotch Express leaving Carlisle Station.

underground gallery, housing the cathedral's treasures – ancient copes, historic plate, books and silver, plus displays that tell the story of Christian Cumbria.

Next door is the very good Undercroft Buttery and a bookshop. Sir Walter Scott got married here on Christmas Eve 1797 to a local Cumbrian girl, Charlotte Carpenter – in fact, her father was French, but she had become the ward of a Cumbrian lord.

✳

Carlisle's classic Victorian cemetery, dating back to 1855, is one of Cumbria's hidden treasures. On the southern outskirts of the city, it covers over 38 hectares with chapels and ancient gravestones, plus hills, woods, streams and bridges with wild orchids, wild violets, butterflies and dragonflies. It was one of the first cemeteries in Britain to introduce woodland burials, the graves being marked by an oak tree. In 2008 it was named the UK's cemetery of the year for the third year running. In 2014 a pretty little café was opened in the Grade II-listed main entrance to the cemetery in Richardson Street. Not many cemeteries turn themselves into tourist attractions. People now visit the cemetery not just to remember loved ones, but also to enjoy a large nature reserve and to admire the Victorian monuments.

✳

If you can bear to drag yourself away from wonderful Carlisle and travel five miles south, you'll find the village of Wreay, which has a unique (not to say eccentric) church with a rectangular nave and a semicircular apse, following the style of Roman basilicas. Coming across it so near to Carlisle you might imagine you have wandered into Tuscany or southern Germany. It's a handmade church, in the sense that it was built and designed by one person, Sarah Losh, between 1840 and 1842. She was the daughter of a local family – clever and talented and well connected.

Main Street in Cockermouth.

3012. Main Street, Cockermouth.

Dante Gabriel Rossetti described the church as 'extraordinary architectural works' with 'a Byzantine style and other things. . . full of beauty and imaginative detail, though extremely severe and simple' and 'much more original than the things done by the young architects now'.

Over the years Sarah Losh has been largely forgotten, but a recent prize-winning book, *The Pinecone* by Jenny Uglow, has brought her back to national attention. She even has her own fanclub, the Sarah Losh Society, which has regular meetings and publications. This is the church all Sarah Losh fans must see.

COCKERMOUTH (population 7,000)

Cockermouth is a fine little town, far easier for parking and everyday shopping than Keswick and distinctly on the way up. Main Street, Market Place and Kirkgate are very attractive and the area around All Saints Church, beside the River Cocker, is pretty. The church, too, is good, although the wall-to-wall carpet looks a bit odd.

Cockermouth has a nice community air about it, the worst aspects of the tourist industry being notably restrained here. Perhaps there are advantages to being outside the National Park after all.

Cockermouth's most famous building today is undoubtedly Wordsworth House (see page 177), a fine Georgian building at the end of the main street – which is called Main Street, just to help you find it.

Cockermouth's other notable building is the castle, built originally in the thirteenth century, though most of what remains dates from 100 years later. Much of it is in ruins, but until recently part of it was still lived in by the Egremont family. It's very rarely open to the public, but there's a good view of the walls from beside the river.

There's no theatre or cinema here – although the enterprising Kirkgate Centre has films and shows – and no rail links. Just when I was about to say that the town has been well cleared and cleaned up after the awful floods of 2009 along came the awful floods of December 2015.

A lot more of the Georgian gems have been prettily painted these days, particularly in Market Place and Kirkgate. Lots of good tea and coffee places, too, plus antique shops, excellent veggie dinners at Quince & Medlar, auction rooms at Mitchells and a good art gallery, Castlegate, specialising in northern and Scottish artists.

GRANGE-OVER-SANDS (population 4,000)

Cumbria's riviera – according to the tourist-board people, who have cunningly photographed it to include Grange's solitary palm tree swaying in the breeze. It is a Victorian town, genteel and once a popular holiday resort. If the beach was better, it might have become another Blackpool. As it is, it tends to be popular mostly as a retirement town (known locally as 'the waiting room'), though the choice may seem an odd one, as Grange is famous for its hills. The town is largely unspoilt and seems to be made entirely of grey limestone. Behind the town, on Hampsfell, is a spectacular limestone escarpment, now protected but once quarried extensively for building houses and walls. On the escarpment is a peculiar limestone structure known as Hampsfell Hospice, built for the 'shelter and entertainment' of wanderers over the fell. The view from here on a clear day is fantastic – from Blackpool Tower to Skiddaw.

The sands across to Morecambe Bay are very dangerous, although there is a highway – if you know where to look for it – and the official guide takes parties across. The beach is unsuitable for swimming (although there is the occasional windsurfer) and has been rather spoilt by the railway line, which cuts between the beach and the town. A good promenade.

KENDAL (population 23,000)

Visitors to Kendal have suffered in the last few years with its fiendish one-way system. Take a navigator to make notes of likely parking places as you are swept past them, then aim for them on the second time around. It is a shame, because Kendal is a busy market town and is quite lively culturally, largely thanks to the Brewery Arts Centre. The best parts of Kendal are Kirkland (right at the end of the main shopping street and often referred to as Kirkland Village), and the small lanes known as 'yards' off the main street. In the town centre are two shopping developments – the larger Westmorland Shopping Centre makes much use of local stone and natural lighting. Kendal used to be the largest town in the old county of Westmorland, and is now the administrative centre for the Lake District Special Planning Board.

There was once a Roman fort just south of the town, called Alauna. Kendal suffered from the Scots (like everywhere else) but settled down a little during the fourteenth century and became famous for Kendal Green, a heavy cloth advertised by Shakespeare in *Henry IV*. The castle, which stands on the hill to the east of the River Kent, was built by William Rufus and once belonged to Thomas Parr. His daughter, Katherine, later achieved fame as one of the wives of Henry VIII. Today it is a ruin, but commands a fine view over the town.

Kendal has its own railway station in the heart of the town, a branch connected to the mainline at Oxenholme, which is technically a mainline station but is hardly more than a halt.

Those of you who are thinking, 'But what about Kendal Mint Cake?' hurry to page 301.

*

Abbot Hall, an immaculate Georgian building, is at the southern end of Kendal, just behind the parish church, and has one of the most attractive settings in town – right by the river and looking up towards Kendal Castle. Kendal might be a small, provincial town, but this is not another small, provincial gallery. It is generally reckoned to be the finest art gallery in the Northwest and one of the top twenty in the whole country.

Abbot Hall was built in 1759 for Lt.-Col. George Wilson (at a cost of £8,000). Opened as an art gallery in 1962, it was restored to the decorative splendour of the 1760s in 1992. Downstairs it houses a small but impressive collection of eighteenth- and nineteenth-century paintings, including several by George Romney, displayed along with period furniture, porcelain and glassware. Upstairs the house becomes a more traditional art gallery with displays of works by Barbara Hepworth, Ben Nicholson and L. S. Lowry. In 1996 a Lucian Freud exhibition attracted 20,000 visitors, and the exhibition got rave reviews in the national press, on TV and radio. Who needs London?

*

Next door, housed in what used to be Abbot Hall's stable block, is the Museum of Lakeland Life and Industry. Part of the collection spills over into the adjacent seventeenth-century grammar school. It won the first ever Museum of the Year Award in 1973. Most of the exhibits are on open display – you

Stricklandgate, Kendal c. 1880.

can touch them, walk round them, peer under them, even sniff them if you want to. Some of the drawers are worth opening, too. It's a fantastic little museum, full of reconstructed workshops with genuine, hand-worn tools and instruments. There's a beautiful old nineteenth-century printing press, made of cast iron and once used by the *Westmorland Gazette*, and a bedroom and living room, fully furnished as they might have been around 1900. This is definitely the best museum for anyone interested in Lakeland and its people.

There is also a replica of Arthur Ransome's study, with many of his possessions, including his desk and typewriter. In 2015, the displays in the Ransome Room were expanded to include material from the museum's archive given by Ransome's second wife, Evgenia Shelepina, who was working as Trotsky's secretary when Ransome met her in Russia. They include the

The Brush Factory in Kendal
c. 1910.

first book that Ransome wrote at the age of six and sketchbooks for the *Swallows and Amazons* series.

Part of the attraction of the Museum of Lakeland Life is its minimal use of labels and text, but this can have its drawbacks – quite often you find yourself wondering what on earth you're looking at. The only remedy is to arm yourself with the guide book before you go in and think of it as part of the admission fee, or use the 'Listening Posts', one of which teaches you to count in Cumbrian dialect.

*

Not far south of Kendal are two stately homes that are well worth a visit. Sizergh Castle, close to the A591, was the home of the Strickland family for 700 years. There was an original house on the site, but this was replaced in 1340 with a pele tower. Those Scots again. It's the largest tower in Cumbria that's still standing (if you don't count factory towers). The great hall was added in 1450 and some very fine panelling and carving in Elizabethan times; the gardens date from the eighteenth century. Sizergh is owned and run by the National Trust, so you'll find the inevitable shop.

Another mile or two further south, by Levens Bridge, is Levens Hall, a magnificent Elizabethan mansion, owned and lived in by the Bagot family. It began life as a Norman pele tower, and has some fine paintings, furniture and plasterwork, and a fascinating fireplace in the south drawing room with carvings depicting the four seasons, the four elements and the five senses.

Levens offers the usual special events and attractions to bring in the kiddies on bank holidays, such as steam trains, but the standout attraction at Levens is the topiary garden, laid out in 1694 by the French gardener of King James II.

MARYPORT (population 11,000)

Maryport was originally a village called Ellenfoot, till Humphrey Senhouse developed the port in the eighteenth century and called it after his wife Mary.

So sweet. Maryport is the birthplace of Thomas Ismay, founder of the White Star Line, who built the *Titanic*.

Today, it's a smaller but somehow sadder version of Whitehaven, despite all that development in the harbour. The plans are exciting, the new buildings architecturally interesting, the new marina attractive, but much of the harbour still looks like a wasteland. There's a small maritime museum by the quay, awfully neat and attractive, run on a shoestring budget using enthusiasm and invention rather than the latest wonder-display techniques. In the town itself, head for the cobbled Fleming Square, walk on to the Senhouse Roman Museum, down the cliff and back along the promenade. You'll probably meet no one.

*

Senhouse Roman Museum is one of the country's least known yet one of the oldest and most interesting private collections of Roman relics. It was begun in 1570 by John Senhouse, who collected bits from the old Roman fort at Maryport, and it continued through twelve generations of his family. It was finally opened to the public in 1990 in a converted Victorian naval battery overlooking the town. The museum has just three rooms, but take them slowly if you want to savour the sexual undertones in items such as the Serpent Stone, probably Celtic and what a big one – a phallus over five feet high – or the 'Pin-up Girl', a naked girl carved in stone to welcome soldiers going on leave. Naff modern paintings showing Roman life make you realise just how artistically gifted those Romans were.

PENRITH (population 12,000)

A sandstone-built market town on the eastern fringes of the Lake District. Its character is rather muted, and spoilt by traffic during the week. A little overlooked and forgotten compared with Carlisle, but a nice, friendly place for shopping. One of its best attractions is the view from Penrith Beacon, which stands on a hill overlooking the town. It gives a superb view west across the plain to the Lakeland Fells.

Like Carlisle, its history goes back to Roman times but then got overrun by the marauding Scots once the Romans had gone. An unusual castle, originally merely a defensive tower, was built around 1400 and enlarged in subsequent years, falling into disuse during the sixteenth century and providing a stock of building material for the local houses. The castle was a favourite dwelling of Richard, duke of Gloucester (later Richard III), when he was warden of the West Marches. The oldest and most interesting buildings are to be found around the church, most of which date from the 1700s.

William and Dorothy Wordsworth went to school in Penrith for a time, and in later life William wrote of the town's famous Beacon. This structure was once a link in a communication chain that ran the length of the country and was a useful early-warning system when the Scots were on the rampage again.

Penrith makes a good base for exploring both Lakeland and the Eden Valley. It has a mainline railway station, though London–Glasgow trains don't always bother to stop, which means using Carlisle or Oxenholme – if, of course, they bother to stop there. Oh, all these decisions. The castle – now in ruins – is open to the public and lies in the public park.

The area around St Andrew's Church is very attractive. There is a cinema, which is nothing special and lags behind those in Bowness and Ambleside. There are two olde worlde shops at either end of Market Square, which have somehow survived for over 200 years. Graham's, the posh grocers, is Penrith's answer to Fortnum & Mason. Very county. Arnison, the drapers, established in 1740, once the home of Wordsworth's grandparents, is in a magnificent time warp. Not so long ago there was still a sticker on the front door announcing 'We stock nylons'.

Penrith Museum, which is tacked on to the Tourist Information Centre in Middlegate, is a very modest place, but the ancient building that houses the museum, Robinson's School, is interesting, and the museum gives you an

excuse to poke around inside. It was a school at one time, a charitable foundation for poor girls, then became the tourist centre. Since 1990 it has also housed the town's local history museum, with photos, documents and artefacts about Penrith's history and assorted worthies. It's of little interest to outsiders, and probably pretty boring for most Penrithians too.

*

There are plenty of things to do and see close to Penrith, including two good ruined castles close to the southern outskirts of the town: Brougham Castle, close to where the River Eamont joins the River Lowther, is well preserved – for a ruin. It was once a very important castle built within the ramparts of a Roman fort, and was one of the many castles restored by Lady Anne Clifford in the seventeenth century. By the time Turner painted it in its riverside setting it had fallen into disrepair. It is now run by English Heritage.

Brougham Hall, a mile or so southwest along the Lowther, looks like a castle, feels like a castle, but is really a stately home that dates back 500 years and has been visited by many royals. It was once the home of Henry Brougham, 1st Baron Brougham and Vaux, who was Lord Chancellor in the 1830s and gave his name to the light, four-wheeled, horse-drawn Brougham carriage. The house has now been restored by a charity and houses various crafts and workshops. It's pronounced 'broom', as in what you sweep a floor with.

Southwest of Penrith is Rheged – Cumbria's newest, biggest, highly popular and most impressive manmade tourist attraction. Despite all that, it's easy to miss, as it's cunningly grass-covered and built into a hill, just two minutes from Junction 40 on the M6, beside the roundabout, as if heading to Keswick. Rheged was the name for Cumbria's ancient Celtic Kingdom, so the main aim, in theory, is to introduce you to the wonders of Cumbria. But it is also a retail experience, with lots of shops and eating places and families wandering around, though there are local arts and crafts here as well.

An engraving of Penrith Castle.

ULVERSTON (population 11,000)

Ulverston is a typical friendly northern market town (great on Thursdays) with a market cross, nice old cobbled streets and a nearby canal. Overlooking the town is the monument to Sir John Barrow – a 90-foot-high imitation of the Eddystone Lighthouse, which is a feature of the landscape that can be seen for miles. There is a public path up Hoad Hill leading to the monument, and from this vantage there are good views of the town and surrounding countryside.

Ulverston may seem like an unlikely place to have 'the world's largest collection of Laurel and Hardy memorabilia', but that's only if you didn't know that Stan Laurel was born Arthur Stanley Jefferson in Ulverston on 16 June 1890 (Stan Laurel was his stage name). The museum was set up by L&H fanatic (and one-time Mayor of Ulverston) Bill Cubin. There is tons of stuff: posters, letters, portraits, possessions. You can even see L&H films – the collection has virtually every one available and shows them continually. The museum was originally tucked away in Bill's storeroom in the town, but in 2009 it moved to the stage of the old Roxy Cinema in Brogden Street (the 2009 opening was performed by Ken Dodd). Outside on the pavement is a life-sized bronze of Laurel and Hardy with their little dog, Laughing Gravy, nipping away at their heels. People smile just looking at it.

If you can make it to Backbarrow, five or so miles up the road towards Windermere, you'll find the Lakeland Motor Museum, which relocated from Grange-over-Sands to the site of the former Reckitt's Blue Dye Works carton-packaging sheds in 2010. It houses a collection of over eighty historic vehicles – cars, motorbikes, cycles, engines – as well as around 20,000 smaller motoring bits and pieces, such as illuminated petrol-pump signs, toy cars, a walk-round 1920s garage and Princess Margaret's scooter. They also have an East German Trabant, driven over when the Berlin Wall came down.

*

Just outside Ulverston is Swarthmoor Hall, an Elizabethan manor house built around 1586. George Fox, principal founder of the Quakers, first came to preach here in 1652 and later married Margaret Fell, whose home it was. The manor became the powerhouse of the Quaker movement. (Swarthmoor in the USA is named after the house.) It was bought by the Society of Friends (i.e. the Quakers) in 1954 and is now used for educational and residential purposes.

Six rooms can be seen, containing Quaker and non-Quaker furniture, books (including a wonderful 1541 Tudor Bible) and other items. But best of all is the house itself.

*

Conishead Priory, on the Furness peninsula near Ulverston, is a stunning-looking building – and it is also rather stunning to find that it is inhabited by a Buddhist community. 'There is no house in England like Conishead,' according to Simon Jenkins in his book *England's Thousand Best Houses*. He was obviously amazed to come across such a building in such an out-of-the-way corner of England. English Heritage has also given it good reviews, describing it as 'a very important Gothic Revival country house with few peers in the Northwest; the distinctive two towers of the front elevation are an important local landmark'.

The priory dates back to the twelfth century and has played an import-ant role in the life of the local community for centuries, but not always as a religious centre. Since 1976 it has been home to an international college for Buddhist studies. When the Buddhist community moved in, the priory had lain empty for four years and was entirely derelict and close to collapse. Over the past three decades Manjushri Buddhist Centre has raised almost £1 million and invested thousands of hours of voluntary labour to eradicate dry rot. Now it has been restored it receives thousands of visitors each year who admire all the turrets and spires, cloisters, massive stained-glass windows and wood panelling. There are seventy acres of wooded grounds, which you can wander round, going all the way down to the shore of Morecambe Bay. The Buddhists – very friendly folk – allow you into the house and grounds at weekends all summer, and don't even charge, unless you go on a conducted tour.

*

A short drive away from Ulverston, in a small valley midway between Barrow-in-Furness and Dalton, is Furness Abbey. It was mentioned by Wordsworth, and is now a ruin in the care of English Heritage (the two facts are not connected). The remains are very impressive, with some parts almost at their original height. The abbey dates from around 1127 and the layout can be clearly seen – in sections. The walls rear overhead and you get the powerful feeling of the monastery's size and influence.

WHITEHAVEN (population 26,000)

While Cockermouth and Penrith have crept into Lakeland and been accepted as 'one of us', the west-coast towns have long been considered out of sight, if not off the map. Few tourists will linger long in Barrow unless visiting the Dock Museum or trying to find Furness Abbey or Piel Island. And they won't find much to detain them in Workington, apart from Portland Square.

But hurry, hurry to Whitehaven, before everyone else discovers it. At the moment, it's a tourist-free zone, offering visitors the chance to mingle with genuine Cumbrians.

In the eighteenth century, Whitehaven was the nation's third port, after London and Bristol, rich on coal exports and tobacco imports. The Georgian town had been laid out on a grid pattern by the Lowther family, the first planned town in Britain. George Washington's granny lived in Whitehaven. John Paul Jones, founder of the American navy, raided the town in 1778.

After some dismal decades of decline in the shipping and coal industries, Whitehaven has come to life again. You can see it in the spruced-up Georgian

An invoice from stationer's and paper bag manufacturers W. H. Moss & Sons in Whitehaven.

streets and squares. It's not all handouts and guilt money from Sellafield, but civic pride and a new, if gentler, affluence. The Georgian bit is towards the harbour – Lowther Street, King Street, Roper Street. Once you've worked out the one-way streets and managed to park, you can explore all the delights on foot. Pause a while to read the monster mosaic poem in the Market Place, then you can go to Michael Moon's amazing bookshop and compliment him. (He wrote the verse.)

Probably the biggest, best attraction of Whitehaven for all visitors is the huge harbour front, now a conservation area. Walk out on Sir John Rennie's West Pier till you're almost halfway to America, touch the sandstone blocks, then look back and think of England. Indoor delights include the Beacon Museum (in a handsome modern building, shaped like a lighthouse, on Whitehaven harbour), which covers the town's social, maritime and industrial history, and also the Rum Museum in a 1785 bonded warehouse on Lowther Street. Culture can be had at Rosehill Theatre. Don't forget St Bees just down the coast.

If you can make it five miles south of Whitehaven you could visit the castle at Egremont, in a public park at the south end of the town. It stands on a mound in a loop of the River Ehen and has some stylish herringbone masonry. Egremont is also the home of the Egremont Crab Fair and Sports, venue of the World Gurning Championships (see page 288).

(see page 288)

*

The Haig Colliery, up on the cliffs above Whitehaven, is one of the few proper leftovers from the coal-mining industry that dominated West Cumberland for centuries. It is scarcely remembered today, now that the pitheads and slag heaps have been flattened; in most west-coast villages the pitmen's terraced houses and memorials to the miners who died are the only evidence that remains.

In the 1950s, there were 1,800 working in this pit, some of them 2,000 feet down and four miles out to sea. The pit was left derelict when it finally closed in 1986 – still with fourteen dead miners entombed from a 1927 disaster. In 1994, a voluntary organisation began restoring the buildings, machinery and engines, and the Haig Pit Mining and Colliery Museum opened in 1997.

MY FAVOURITE LAKELAND TOWN

Whitehaven is the town I most enjoy visiting when we are in Lakeland. It happens to be handy for us in Loweswater, and is never very busy; parking is easy, the walks excellent, the local life real and genuine. In fact, I have been heard to declare that Whitehaven is not just my favourite town in West Cumbria, but in all Cumbria, in all England – nay, in the whole of the United Kingdom, even Europe.

'Better than Venice?' said my wife. 'Or Paris? You do say such stupid things.'

Look, just keep out of it, pet. Anyway, I said favourite, which is my subjective opinion, and Paris is a city not a town.

My early memories of it are sitting on the back of the team coach coming back from Whitehaven having been hammered, when I played for Carlisle Grammar School First XV, boaster. We always got thumped when we played Whitehaven Grammar School. And, in fact, by every other school in Cumbria. Our only 'foreign' trip was away to Newcastle Royal Grammar School, but they would only let us play their second team – who thumped us even more than Whitehaven did. Not that we cared much. We considered ourselves artists, me and my friend Reginald Hill, not thugs.

Forty years ago, driving across from a cottage we used to have at Caldbeck, Whitehaven seemed a dull, dismal, rundown sort of place, which had lost its industrial identity but not yet found a new role. Since we moved to Loweswater in 1986 and began to visit it more frequently, I have been able to observe the most remarkable transformation. Mainly, of course, it's been the harbour; what an achievement, what an amazing success they have made of it. I really do think it is the most attractive, interesting, historic harbour in all Cumbria, in all England. . . Sorry, sorry, it just slipped out.

I honestly never do tire of walking round it, whatever the weather – in rain it has its own moody, misty atmosphere. I either go to the end of all the stone piers in turn, or try to time it so I get a round walk, hoping that the walkway over the new harbour gates is open. Or I just walk around the quayside, perhaps have some tapas – that well-known old Cumbrian delicacy – at Zest by the harbour, if it's not too busy.

The main Zest, a much posher restaurant, is on the way out of town. We usually go after visiting St Bees, finishing off a perfect day. I look upon St Bees as part of Whitehaven, as it's just round the corner, and I check the tides before I go there, so I can walk the whole beach, up the little cliff, round the golf course, back through St Bees itself to the beach caff. I love that as well – so unsmart, utilitarian, honest, reliable, and with great views. It's my bestest outing, on which I drag all visitors – Whitehaven plus St Bees. All my children and grandchildren do the same, insisting on a Whitehaven–St Bees outing.

After the harbour, it's the Georgian streets and buildings that make Whitehaven so special. I was never aware of them as a lad, but they must have been there, being Georgian – I'm not *that* old. When you're young, you tend not to notice architecture – even we artists in the Carlisle Grammar School sixth form. But the other reason is that, in recent decades, Georgian Whitehaven has been cleaned up, saved, preserved, painted and lovingly cared for. You now can't help but notice and admire.

My pudding, the treat I save for last, is a visit to Michael Moon's second-hand bookshop in Lowther Street. He has over 60,000 books and one mile of shelving. When Michael Moon doesn't know where things are, which is often, he will always try to amuse you with a stream of stories.

He's been almost forty years in the bookselling business, and with a prominent position in the middle of Whitehaven, with a large shop front, he's got used to idiots – I mean, customers – coming in with dopey requests. Last time I was in his shop, he'd put up a notice listing things he does NOT sell. String vests, broccoli, loofahs, home perm-kits, galvanized mop buckets, Manx kippers and knitted toilet roll holders – for example.

I thought it was all genuine at first, with its period typography and layout, but on closer examination I suspect he has made up a few items. He insists, however, that all of them are based on real goods that used to be sold locally. Once upon a time. . .

Eleven Villages Worth A Detour

No visitor to Lakeland should restrict themselves to the main touristy honeypots and the larger towns. The Lake District is as rich in villages that are lovely or fascinating (or both) as any region of England. Here are eleven such places, some of them (like Hesket Newmarket) a little off the beaten track, some of them (like Cartmel) increasingly trendy and sought-after.

ASKHAM

Askham is an ancient and pretty village a few miles south of Penrith. Many houses here date from between 1650 and 1750. Askham Hall is fourteenth century in parts and was developed on the site of a pele tower. Lowther Castle has long only been a facade, mostly ruins, but is now being rebuilt and re-landscaped (see page 271). But the Lowther family has occupied the land around here for hundreds of years, and there were a couple of earlier buildings on the site of the present castle.

BROUGHTON-IN-FURNESS

On the southern boundary of the National Park, close to the Duddon Estuary, Broughton considers itself a market town, but it's really a large village. Most of it was built in the eighteenth century and the market square has hardly changed in the last two centuries. You can still see the old stone fish slabs.

Broughton has been, and still is, largely missed by the tourist hordes, which means it is a nice little place, unspoilt and friendly. The obelisk in the square was erected to commemorate the jubilee of George III in 1810.

To the north of the village is Broughton Tower, which was once an old pele tower. The Broughton family's association with this area dates back to before the Norman Conquest. The name 'Broughton' means 'the hamlet by the stream', the '–in-Furness' bit being added later to distinguish the village from the other Broughtons dotted about the North and Northwest of England.

CALDBECK

As Grasmere is to Wordsworth, so Caldbeck, in its own little way, is to John Peel, the famous huntsman and hero of the song 'D'ye Ken John Peel' (see page 263). Set near open fells to the 'Back o' Skiddaw', on the northern boundary of the National Park, it has a traditional village green, duck pond, a twelfth-century church and an amazing river gorge and waterfall called the Howk. Look out for the signs, if you can find them.

The churchyard holds the bodies of two famous Lakeland characters: John Peel and Mary Robinson, the Beauty of Buttermere (see pages 263–5). Caldbeck is a real, working village, not yet overrun by tourists, despite a gift shop in a barn. It is also the home of the mountaineer Chris Bonington.

*

A few miles south of Caldbeck, on the southeastern side of Carrock Fell, is the tiny hamlet of Mosedale. In 1653 the Quaker George Fox came to preach here, and later a Meeting House was built in Mosedale, which still stands today. It's been exquisitely restored and, although small and humble – just one room – it's well worth stopping for, especially in the summer when they serve rather nice teas. The Quakers have strong roots in Cumbria, dating back to George Fox's early years. (He married Margaret Fell of Swarthmoor Hall, Ulverston; see page 159.)

CARTMEL

A lovely little village, just west of Grange-over-Sands, with a beautiful square, an old village pump still standing and a nice river, the Eea, running through it. Very popular on Sunday lunchtimes, as it contains a number of good pubs (the King's Arms and the Cavendish Arms). Cartmel is a bit picture-book, but it is still less of an open museum than Hawkshead (see pages 139–40).

Cartmel used to be most famous for its priory, which dates back to 1188, when it was founded by William Marshall, the baron of Cartmel. Nothing

An engraving of the Grange in Borrowdale by John Farington, 1815.

now remains of the original priory except the gatehouse (owned by the National Trust) and church. The gatehouse is open to the public, just off Cartmel Square. The church has been restored several times and is now a collection of styles; the east window is fifteenth century. The best features are the carved oak misericords, with some delightful mermaids, apes, elephants and unicorns.

But now Cartmel has put itself on the national map thanks to L'Enclume, Simon Rogan's Michelin-starred restaurant, which has regularly been voted the best thing ever, anywhere.

*

Cartmel is home to probably the smallest of the National Hunt courses, set at the opposite end of the village to the priory. There are race meetings on the late spring and summer bank holidays, with other race days sandwiched in between. Cartmel Racecourse and its grandstand may be small, but race days attract big crowds. Cumbria Crystal Cup Day, in July, features Cartmel's most valuable race, the Cumbria Crystal Cup being worth more than £25,000.

As well as the horse racing, on race days there is usually a small fairground along with stalls and refreshment tents.

*

Just a mile or so southwest of Cartmel, and a quarter of a mile's walk from the railway station at Cark-in-Cartmel, is Holker Hall – an outstanding country house owned by the Cavendish family, dating back to the seventeenth century and set in a 120-acre park. The site itself used to belong to Cartmel Priory. Holker Hall contains some beautiful examples of panelling and wood-carving and some rare paintings, including works by Anthony van Dyck and Joshua Reynolds. It is a traditional 'stately home', but without ropes and restrictions. The gardens are wonderful and contain what is said to be the oldest monkey puzzle tree in the country.

There's usually a lot going on at Holker, as the owners, like most stately home proprietors, have to find amusing and remunerative ways to bring in the punters, so they have held things like model aircraft rallies, hot-air ballooning, vintage car rallies. All very professionally done, but if you want to see the house and grounds at their best, go when none of these wonders are on. The gardens are best in early summer.

GRANGE-IN-BORROWDALE

One of Lakeland's prettiest villages, Grange was once a grange of Furness Abbey. It's only a small hamlet but is beautifully situated alongside the River Derwent, south of Derwentwater.

The novelist Hugh Walpole (see page 238) lived in Brackenburn, a large house about a mile north of here, from 1924 until his death in 1941.

HESKET NEWMARKET

A northern hamlet well off the tourist beat. Once an important market, now it is just a pleasant village built around a long green. Hesket Hall is a dull but odd building with a peculiar roof and twelve angular projections forming the walls. The corners of these projections are supposed to make an effective sundial. There's a good pub here, the Old Crown, run as a co-op with its own real ale.

Charles Dickens and Wilkie Collins stayed at the Queen's Head Inn at Hesket Newmarket (now a private house) in 1857, and went on an ill-advised expedition to climb Carrock Fell, getting caught in rain and mist. They described their tour of the area in *The Lazy Tour of Two Idle Apprentices*.

But forget Dickens – Hesket Newmarket was the birthplace of the great Eddie Stobart (see pages 274–6).

MAULDS MEABURN

Not in the Lake District proper, as it's across the M6, towards Appleby, but many discriminating Cumbrians consider it the county's prettiest village.

A postcard of Buttermere
and Crummock Water.

Fascinating stone houses, each one different, on either bank of the River Lyvennet.

PATTERDALE AND GLENRIDDING

Two rather shapeless villages at the southern end of Ullswater, separated by less than a mile. Patterdale is the prettier and more of a real village. But the setting is spectacular; they are surrounded on almost all sides by mountains, with the only open view over towards the lake. It is a superb centre for walking, especially for the Striding Edge route up Helvellyn. The name is a corruption of 'Patrick's Dale'. The patron saint of Ireland is supposed to have preached and baptised here. Along the road towards the boat landing at Glenridding you will find St Patrick's Well, which was once thought to have healing properties.

Glenridding was a mining village until the mines closed in 1962. Lead was discovered in the area in the seventeenth century and mining was at its height in the early nineteenth century, when Greenside was one of the best lead mines in the country. Glenridding is best used as a walking centre and as an access to the lake (it is the home of the Ullswater steamers; see page 54).

Seldom Seen is a small row of mining cottages hidden up the valley from Glenridding.

Surrounded by mountains, Patterdale's valley is wet at the best of times, but in December 2015 successive winter storms caused it to experience its worst ever flooding. Water poured off the fells, overwhelmed the gills and becks and inundated the village of Glenridding not once but three times in a fortnight.

ROSTHWAITE

A little hamlet in the Borrowdale Valley, a couple of miles south of Grange (see page 169), useful as a base for setting off for Watendlath, Seatoller, Langstrath and Sty Head. The footpath up to Watendlath used to be quite attractive but is now so wide that it looks like a mini-motorway. . .

TROUTBECK

One of the Lakes' most famous villages. Strung along a hillside just north of Windermere, it is really a series of hamlets grouped together around a number of wells. The cottages and barns date from the seventeenth to nineteenth centuries – the finest of all being Townend, a 1626 statesman's home (this does not mean a politician but rather a more upmarket, more prosperous farmer; see page 310). A dark little place, Townend is run by the National Trust and contains some original and surprisingly elaborate furniture and panelling.

Troutbeck has two old, restored inns, the sign outside the Mortal Man being famous for its rhyme:

> O mortal man that lives by bread,
> What is it makes thy nose so red?
> Thou silly fool that looks so pale,
> 'Tis drinking Sally Birkett's ale.

Note that there is another Lakeland Troutbeck, just off the A66 near Threlkeld. Even Pevsner got the two muddled.

WATENDLATH

A moorland hamlet of farms between the Borrowdale and Thirlmere valleys, set artistically beside a large tarn. It is situated to the east of Rosthwaite and was the remote, isolated setting for Hugh Walpole's novel *Judith Paris*. Watendlath is now a magnet for tourists and is best avoided on summer bank holidays. It can be reached by leaving the B5289 between Keswick and Rosthwaite and crossing Ashness Bridge. This road is a menace in the high season and it is better to leave the car and walk.

5

Wordsworth and the Lake Poets

After breakfast I accompanied Mr Wordsworth and
his family to Grasmere Church… , it was delightful
to observe with what mingled respect and familiarity
our group was saluted by all the peasants.

'PHILIP KEMPFERHAUSEN', 1818

THERE ARE THOSE WHO ASSUMED, BACK IN THE NINETEENTH century, and still assume today, that it was the Lake Poets who really put Lakeland on the map – by raving about it and making it sound like an awfully desirable, attractive place for those of a sensitive, artistic, discerning nature to visit.

But it is true that for a long period in the Victorian era Lakeland became a centre of English literary life, at least its poetic parts, with Robert Southey becoming Poet Laureate in 1813 and then on his death in 1843 being succeeded by Wordsworth.

The group of writers known as the Lake Poets not only wrote about the Lakes, but also became a Lakeland attraction in their own right; visitors flocked to places they had written about, houses they were living in or had lived in, hoping for a sight of the great men. Many books and booklets were produced about the homes of the poets, or places and personages associated with them, which were still being published long after they had moved on to meet their maker – or died, as we say in non-poetic circles.

There were women poets and novelists and writers who lived in Lakeland and wrote about Lakeland, whom we will come to later, but those we call the Lake Poets were all men. In the 1840s, the number-one Lakeland literary celebrity was Wordsworth. And it was to his house at Rydal Mount, near Ambleside, that literary groupies headed, hoping, just hoping, not only to catch a glimpse of the grand old man, but to acquire a lock of his hair too.

What happened at Rydal Mount was that a gardener, who often used to cut Wordsworth's hair, would lean over the wall when he saw fans and rubbernecks approaching and say, 'Psst, anyone fancy a lock of the Poet Laureate's hair? I'm not asking shillings, I'm not asking pennies – yours for a farthing, but don't let on.'

WILLIAM WORDSWORTH (1770–1850)

Wordsworth really was a Lakelander born and bred, a true Cumbrian – unlike almost all of the other writers we now associate with the Lakes, such as Beatrix

PREVIOUS SPREAD
An engraving of Grasmere Lake by John Laporte, 1795.

Potter, Arthur Ransome, John Ruskin, Hugh Walpole and Alfred Wainwright, all of whom were 'offcomers', born and raised elsewhere, who only arrived and settled in Lakeland as adults.

Wordsworth was born in Cockermouth on 7 April 1770, the second eldest in a family of five. His father John was a lawyer who worked as a steward for Sir James Lowther, one of the richest landowners in the North of England. Wordsworth House, in the main street of Cockermouth, was, and still is, the handsomest house in that very pretty West Cumbrian town. You can go round it today and admire its beautiful Georgian front and imposing gate piers, inspect the fine rooms and furniture (much of it owned by Wordsworth himself), and look at the excellent portraits of Wordsworth and the other Lakes writers. There's even a fine landscape by J. M. W. Turner, who once stayed at Cockermouth Castle with his patron, Lord Egremont. But the house itself was never owned by the Wordsworths. It came with the job and was always owned by the Lowther family.

The precise financial relationship between John Wordsworth and the Lowthers has never been made clear. From the records it looks as if John Wordsworth never paid any rent. At the same time, he didn't get much of a salary, if any. He worked himself into an early grave for the Lowther family and got very little for his trouble. Sir James Lowther controlled nine parliamentary seats and one of Wordsworth's father's jobs was to go round at election time, keeping the voters sweet with money and other favours. He had a small property of his own, which brought in a small income. He was also coroner of Millom, a position he got through Lowther influence.

Wordsworth's mother was Ann Cookson, daughter of a linen draper in Penrith, on the east side of Cumberland. The Cooksons lived over the shop in the market square. They had some landed relations and considered themselves as belonging to the 'Penrith upper classes', despite being only shopkeepers. Penrith, then as now, is a little market town with a decided lack of upper-class folk, though the surrounding area is still rich in squirearchy and fine estates.

William Wordsworth
(1770–1850)

William went for a time to school in Cockermouth, where one of the pupils was Fletcher Christian, of *Mutiny on the Bounty* fame. The Christians were neighbours of the Wordsworths in Cockermouth. (It's interesting to note that during this period Cockermouth, for all its smallness and isolation, produced three people who, in completely different ways, went on to gain national recognition – the other being John Dalton, who produced the theory of the atom in 1808.)

There are few records of Wordsworth's school days in Cockermouth, but quite a lot about the dame school he later attended in Penrith, his mother's hometown. At this school William and Dorothy, his only sister, who was twenty-one months younger, became close friends of the Hutchinson children.

From his mother, Wordsworth was taught a love of the countryside and they went on picnics and expeditions to places like the Penrith Beacon, the local landmark. Wordsworth's father is a more shadowy figure, forever travel-

A postcard of Hawkshead School, which Wordsworth attended as a boy.

ling round Cumberland on his master's business, but he taught Wordsworth to learn chunks of Milton and Shakespeare by heart and introduced him to the novels of Henry Fielding.

Wordsworth was unhappy with his Penrith relations, with whom he was forced to spend so much of his early years. They had aspirations to gentility and considered him wild and unruly, too full of animal spirits. Even his own mother found him a handful and predicted that William would be memorable – 'either for good or evil'. Dorothy, in later years, remembered many tears being associated with their time in Penrith and how their uncles disliked William.

It all got worse in 1778 when William was almost eight and his mother died. It looks as if she caught pneumonia, caused, so the family thought, by sleeping on a damp bed while on a visit to London. Dorothy was sent to live with other relations, firstly in Yorkshire, and was very upset to be separated from William. In 1779 William and his brothers were sent away to school at Hawkshead, on the other side of the Lakes, where he was free at last of his Penrith relations and where he found for himself a substitute home.

The little grammar school in Hawkshead had been founded in 1585 by Edwin Sandys, archbishop of York, a native of the parish, and was noted for its scholarship. Education was free, except for an annual entrance fee of one guinea for those who came from outside the immediate area. Twelve local charity boys got everything free, including board and lodgings. The boys ranged from sons of professional people, such as the young Wordsworths, to the sons of humble yeoman farmers. The masters were all clerics, mostly graduates of Cambridge, and there were 100 boys in the school in Wordsworth's time, some having come from as far away as Edinburgh and Hawick, though the great majority were from the valleys and villages of the surrounding Lake District.

Wordsworth and his brothers boarded while at Hawkshead Grammar School with Ann Tyson, a joiner's widow, who looked after the motherless boys with great love and affection. Each boy paid twelve guineas a year for his lodgings, which didn't leave much for many luxuries. Each boy was charged extra for candles, coals, sugar and tea.

Wordsworth was now living in the heart of the Lake District (Penrith and Cockermouth are on the fringes), right beside Esthwaite Water, but also within easy walking distance of Windermere and Coniston. Even at the age of ten, during his first winter in Hawkshead, he was out roaming the fells half the night. He was allowed absolute freedom outside school hours and spent his time fishing, skating on Esthwaite Water, bird watching and stealing birds' eggs. His love of skating stayed with him all his life.

It was during these school years at Hawkshead, between the ages of nine and seventeen, that he first started to have his visions. On his long walks up the valleys and over the fells, he often entered dream-like trances when he felt himself at one with nature. This retreat into a spiritual communion with nature is today thought by some Wordsworth watchers (especially the Freudian ones) to be a direct effect of his mother dying and his unhappy times with his Penrith relations. This state is not uncommon among sensitive adolescents, at least for a while, but it was a state Wordsworth never forgot. He started writing poems at school, encouraged by the headmaster, who was a great lover of poetry. His first known verses were written in 1785 to commemorate the school's bicentenary.

*

In 1783 Wordsworth's father John died. He was riding home at Christmas time from Millom, where he had been conducting an inquest, when he lost his way on Cold Fell, spent the night without shelter on the exposed hillside and never recovered. From then on, not only was Wordsworth an orphan, but he was also beset with endless money problems. His father had died with his affairs hopelessly complicated and with Sir James Lowther (who became the earl of Lonsdale in 1784) owing him £4,700 in legal and political fees. Various uncles took over the guardianship of Wordsworth and his brothers and they tried hard, with no luck, to get the money out of the Lowther family. His relations were strict and severe and still didn't care much for William personally, especially with all that wandering round the fells spouting his own poetry, and he in turn never got on with them. The only nice family event around this period was the rediscovery of Dorothy, during his last year at Hawkshead, whom he met again when she returned to live with their relations in Penrith. They hadn't seen each other for nine years.

In 1787 Wordsworth went up to St John's College, Cambridge. His uncle Richard advanced £400 for his education at Cambridge, a debt that Wordsworth worked hard for many years to repay, not managing to settle it until 1813. Despite going up to Cambridge, he returned to Hawkshead in the holidays, going back to Mrs Tyson and his old digs – the only real home he had. Ann Tyson's account book records the purchase of velvet at 5s 6d and silk at 4s 9d for William, who needed a fine velvet coat for eveningwear at Cambridge.

*

At Cambridge, the image of young William takes on something of a transformation. He had gone up, apparently, as an intense, very serious scholar, miles ahead in Euclid, having promised his guardian, who had forked out the money for his university education, that he would be ordained and then try for a college fellowship, thus ensuring his financial independence. Hawkshead Grammar had a fine tradition of producing such scholars – and Wordsworth's younger brother Christopher became one.

Wordsworth's whole university career is a bit short on detail and surrounded in some mystery, but it is recorded that he quickly dropped mathematics altogether. In his exams in the first term of his first year he was placed in the first class – but from then on he went downhill, preferring to devote himself to other interests. He had the feeling, so he wrote, that at Cambridge he was 'not for that hour, nor for that place'. He violently disliked the compulsory twice-daily chapel attendance and attacked the system, much to the displeasure of his guardians. He was also against competitive examinations. Instead of concentrating on his Latin and Greek, he got himself private lessons in modern Italian. His guardians were naturally incensed, seeing him as a young man wasting his time and their money.

When he arrived back in Hawkshead for his holidays, he was very much the Cambridge dandy, prancing around in his fine clothes, which he refers to in a line in his vast autobiographical poem *The Prelude* – 'my habiliments, the transformation and the gay attire'. He did put on his old clothes when he went back to his former pleasure, walking around the lakes and fells. It was during this holiday time that he began to write 'An Evening Walk', which became his earliest published poem.

At Cambridge he took up dancing and spent a lot of time during his Hawkshead holidays at smart country dances. He would come home at four in the morning, weary with pleasure, and pass the farm workers going to the fields. After one country dance at a farm two miles from Hawkshead, he described the evening as having been a 'promiscuous rout, a medley of all tempers'.

Wordsworth's later image, which he did a lot to encourage by carefully missing out certain early episodes in *The Prelude*, is of a very serious and terribly upright gentleman. But it seems obvious that as a young student he acted very much as so many young students have always acted, running up debts, living a gay social life, disliking the academic system and prancing about in his smart clothes.

*

William Wordsworth didn't return to Hawkshead during his last long vacation at Cambridge. He went off instead with a friend on a three-month 'pedestrian tour' of France, Switzerland and northern Italy. This sort of student trip is commonplace today, at least the backpacking variety, but in 1790 it was rare for young gentlemen to venture off alone around Europe, especially *walking* around Europe. The norm for young gentlemen who wanted the 'grand tour' was to travel in their own coach, or, if they didn't have the money, to get themselves a job as tutor or companion to someone who did have the money and the transport. Wordsworth and his friend set off with £20 between them, a light overcoat each, an oak stick and their belongings in a large pocket handkerchief. Most of their friends thought they were mad. Wordsworth wisely didn't tell his guardians, or even Dorothy, not at least until he had arrived in France.

France was in the first heady stages of Revolution. The Bastille had been stormed and the absolute monarchy put to rout, and Wordsworth and his friend watched many of the celebrations. 'The whole nation was mad with joy,' so Wordsworth wrote to Dorothy. They walked 20 miles a day, joining in the fun at every stop. Like all right-thinking students, they approved of the Revolution and its aims.

In fact, judging by the excitement expressed in his letters to Dorothy, Wordsworth never enjoyed an experience more in his whole life:

> Bliss was it in that dawn to be alive,
> But to be young was very Heaven!

*

Then it was back to England – and to boring old reality. What was Wordsworth going to do for a living? He got his degree in 1791, but a poor one, without honours. He couldn't face the thought of the church or the law, both of which had been vague ideas at one time, so once again doing the full student bit, he bummed around London, spending months cadging beds and meals, doing nothing in particular. Then he bummed around Wales, staying firstly with the Cambridge friend with whom he'd gone walking in Europe. A cousin offered to fix him up with a curacy, but he refused. What he really fancied was being

William Wordsworth's sister, Dorothy.

a tramp, just walking around for ever, if only he could find someone to supply him with £100 a year. 'I am doomed to be an idler through my whole life,' he said in a letter to a friend.

Money problems had hung over him ever since the death of his father. The legal battles continued with Lord Lonsdale, as they tried to get him to pay up the money that the Wordsworth family maintained he owed.

In November 1791 William decided to go back to France, on his own this time, no doubt trying to recapture the good times he had had eighteen months before. This brings us to one of the most intriguing incidents in Wordsworth's life – one that did not become public knowledge until more than a hundred years later, one that you never hear about when you're learning Wordsworth at school.

He went first to Paris, where he watched the Legislative Assembly in action and visited the Jacobin Club, and then in December he moved to Orléans, which in pre-Revolution days had been a popular city where young Englishmen could learn French. He had an introduction to a lady writer living there, but she had gone by the time he arrived. He had very little money, having left England with only £20, but he found some cheap digs in Orléans and got a French girl to give him conversation lessons – for free. The girl was called Annette Vallon, aged twenty-five – four and a half years his senior – and they fell madly in love. She became pregnant and moved back to her home village of Blois.

He followed her to Blois and took digs there secretly, not being exactly popular with Annette's family. In December 1792 Annette moved back to Orléans, presumably because of the displeasure of her family, and it was there that the child she had by William, a girl called Caroline, was born.

But two months before the birth, Wordsworth had gone. He left Annette to go back to England, ostensibly because it was now dangerous to be an Englishman in France, and also hoping that in England the Lonsdale money might have come through, thus allowing him to return and marry and support Annette. However, instead, he went back via Paris. He spent *two months* there, watching and joining in other revolutionary activities, before eventually getting himself back to England.

Was Wordsworth's relationship with Annette just a passing, if rather passionate, affair, which he had no intention of continuing once he was back in England? A case of wild oats being sown by a young student having his first fling? There is no evidence, earlier or later, of Wordsworth being a ladies' man. Did she seduce him? An older woman, picking up an amusing foreign boy? Whatever the circumstances, Wordsworth never forgot Annette, or his commitments. But for the fact that war soon broke out between England and France, and continued for twenty years, save for one brief lull, it seems likely that he would have done the decent thing. If he had done so, his whole life could have turned out very differently.

✳

Annette wrote regularly to William during the war between France and England, but most of the letters were never delivered, though she did not know that at the time. They were confiscated by the French police, since they were sent to a foreign power, and lay in local French archives till they were discovered about 130 years later, which was when the whole story first became public. These letters are very tender and loving, telling him all about his daughter and hoping that very soon he would return and they could be married.

William doesn't appear to have written very often, but he confessed everything to Dorothy on his return and she wrote regularly to Annette, looking upon her as her sister, and Annette wrote to Dorothy in equally loving terms.

Back in England, Wordsworth had a fairly miserable time for the next two or three years. He still had money problems, he was torn between France and England, and his guardians were not very pleased with him. They had probably heard something of the Annette incident, if not of the baby.

He hung around in London and thought at one time of becoming a political journalist, but feared as he suffered from 'nervous headaches' that he wouldn't be able to stand the noise at parliamentary debates. He played a lot of cards, did a lot of late-night talking, wrote away at his poetry and other bits and pieces.

Wordsworth's first poems were published in 1793: *An Evening Walk* (which was set in the Lakes) and 'Descriptive Sketches' (about his pedestrian tour to the continent – the first trip, not his Annette encounter). He hoped to make some money from them, but they sold badly and were not well received, at least by the London critics.

✳

In 1795 Wordsworth decided to leave London. He was disappointed at the reception of his poems and felt the call of the countryside, to live simply and get back to nature. He didn't head for the Lake District, as one might have imagined, but to the West Country, purely because that was where he was offered some free, or very cheap, accommodation. He went with Dorothy, his sister, and they set up house together in Somerset, an idea they'd discussed for many years. Was there a feeling of guilt about the Annette affair and the mess he'd got himself into in France? Did he feel safer with Dorothy? Dorothy, anyway, was absolutely delighted.

It was in Somerset, by chance, that Wordsworth met Samuel Taylor Coleridge and formed a friendship that would become one of the legends of English literature. They came together, dazzled together, shone together like two bright stars, brought out the genius in each other, and even though the fizzling-out stages were to be rather sad, they had an effect on English poetry that has probably never been equalled.

The major result of the friendship of Wordsworth and Coleridge was the appearance of *Lyrical Ballads*, first published anonymously in 1798. The final spur for its publication was the thought of getting money to finance their

Grasmere Lake and village, seen from Hunting Stile.

proposed trip to Germany. They got 30 guineas each for their work, though all but four of the poems were Wordsworth's. Coleridge's main contribution, however, was a substantial one – *The Rime of the Ancient Mariner* (see also page 202). Though it created little fuss at the time, *Lyrical Ballads* is now considered to be one of the turning points in the history of English poetry.

Wordsworth explained that the poems were deliberate experiments, trying to use the language and conversation of ordinary people, writing about ordinary topics, especially the humble and rustic. Many reviewers were outraged by 'The Idiot Boy', but there was general approval for *Tintern Abbey*. It was a complete breakaway, in subject matter and form, from the heavy, metrical poems of the eighteenth century. Wordsworth had been influenced by other contemporary poets – including Robert Burns, whom he greatly admired – but he was showing genuine originality in linking the spiritual with nature, writing personal poetry that had its origins in his own 'emotion recollected in tranquillity'. These early poems had a profound effect on countless young men of the day, who, when they discovered them, suddenly saw a new meaning in language and poetry.

*

In 1799, Wordsworth, aged twenty-nine, decided to return to the Lakes, the inspiration, in subject matter and feelings, of so many of the poems he had written so far. He had decided he wanted to live in Grasmere, the vale of his dreams.

William and Dorothy started the new century in Dove Cottage, Grasmere, having moved in at the end of December 1799. Dove Cottage is known to millions of people round the world as the home of Wordsworth, and every year it attracts around 53,000 visitors – yet the Wordsworths never knew it as Dove Cottage. It didn't have a name when they arrived and they never gave it one. Their address was simply Town End, Grasmere, which was the collective name for the group of cottages at the southern end of the village.

The cottage had at some stage been an inn called the Dove and Olive Branch, and this is where its present-day name came from.

'We were young and healthy and had obtained an object long desired,' wrote Dorothy later. 'We had returned to our native mountains, there to live.' It was a fairly humble cottage, and still is, with two rooms downstairs, plus a back kitchen, and four little rooms above. Dorothy papered one of the little rooms with newspapers to try to keep it warm.

Dorothy and her brother lived there for over eight years and they had a constant stream of relations and visitors who stayed for weeks at a time. Goodness knows where they put them all. Coleridge almost immediately followed them up to the Lakes. He stayed with them in April 1800, and then Dorothy found him a house to let in Keswick, Greta Hall, where he moved in with his family, to be followed not long afterwards by the Southeys.

Coleridge and Southey had married the Fricker sisters, Sarah and Edith, and a third sister also moved into Greta Hall with them. Coleridge, however, seems to have spent most of his time in the first few years with the Wordsworths, walking the thirteen miles or so to take tea, and then staying for weeks at Dove Cottage.

*

The engagement of Wordsworth and Mary Hutchinson happened suddenly – at least that's how it appears in Dorothy's journal. She and William get up one day and head south, making for London. No explanation is given. They cross Westminster Bridge, where Dorothy makes notes of her impressions, which William later turns into one of his finest sonnets. 'Composed upon Westminster Bridge, September 3, 1802' begins with the famous words 'Earth has not anything to show more fair. . .' Oh, and for those of you who are wondering where on earth I've put Wordsworth's 'Daffodils', it's on page 57.

From London, William and Dorothy head for Dover. Where are they going? You've guessed. They're off to see Annette. Now that he has become engaged, William, ever the gentleman, wants Annette to be the first to know. There had been letters back and forth for some years, with Dorothy doing most of the corresponding to Annette. Some of Annette's must have come through, because Dorothy remarks in passing in the journal one day that another letter has come from France. It's safe to assume that William told Mary about his affair with Annette, confessing everything once they got engaged.

The trip to France lasted four weeks in all, and they seem to have spent most of it on the Calais sands. 'We walked by the sea shore almost every evening,' notes Dorothy in her journal, 'with Annette and Caroline, or William and I alone.' It was now August 1802, and the Treaty of Amiens had at last brought a temporary settlement between France and England. William hadn't been to France for ten years or seen his daughter Caroline, who was now ten (unless there was a secret trip during his bumming-around-in-London days). Dorothy gives absolutely nothing away about the nature of the discussions. She describes a few buildings, says that William one day went swimming but that she didn't swim as she had a bad cold, and that's about all.

*

The marriage took place almost immediately after their return from France, in October 1802. Mary's family, the Hutchinsons, weren't too keen on the union, considering William some sort of wandering vagabond with no profession. It was a very quiet affair in Yorkshire, perhaps partly out of consideration to Dorothy. She appears to have been in a state of collapse throughout, and Mary is almost forgotten, as they have to revive Dorothy. In fact, it looks from her own description in her journal as though she couldn't even face the little ceremony:

> At a little after 8 o'clock I saw them go down the avenue to the church. William had parted from me upstairs. I gave him the wedding ring – with how deep a blessing! I took it from my forefinger where

I had worn it the whole of the night before – he slipped it again onto my finger and blessed me fervently. I kept myself as quiet as I could, but when I saw the two men running up the walk, coming to tell us it was over, I could stand it no longer and threw myself on the bed where I lay in stillness neither hearing or seeing anything, till Sara (Mary's sister) came upstairs to me and said, 'They are coming.' This forced me from the bed where I lay and I moved faster than my strength could carry me till I met my Beloved William and fell upon his bosom.

Well, what was all that about? Some academics over the years have suggested that the relationship between William and his sister was incestuous, but there is no proof of that. They were always incredibly close, which must have been hard luck on his wife Mary, but they felt driven together because of what happened to their parents when they were young.

William's marriage to Mary – though never written about to the same degree as his relationship with his sister, mainly because Dorothy was a great letter- and journal-writer – was long and happy and produced five children, though two of them died before the age of ten.

After eight years at Dove Cottage, they moved out – the tenancy being taken over by Thomas De Quincey – and moved to a larger house in Grasmere, Allan Bank, in 1808.

In 1810 Wordsworth and Coleridge became estranged. Coleridge had become an opium addict, among other failings, and Wordsworth now considered him an embarrassment who was sponging off him and being a total pain. Wordsworth was by now a settled and happily married man, a respectable and admired poet who was keeping in with the aristocracy, such as the Lowthers. What caused the split was the leaking of a remark Wordsworth had written to a mutual friend about Coleridge 'being an absolute nuisance in our family', 'a rotten drunkard' who had 'rotted his entrails out by intemperance'. They never met again.

In 1813, Wordsworth was appointed Distributor of Stamps for Westmorland, and the stipend of 400 pounds a year made him financially secure. That same year he and his family, including Dorothy, moved to Rydal Mount, between Grasmere and Ambleside, where he spent the rest of his life.

It was another rented house. In fact, Wordsworth owned none of the houses he ever lived in, from when he was born to when he died. He was appointed Poet Laureate on the death of Southey in 1843. He was now a revered Establishment figure, an upholder of all the right Victorian virtues, someone who appeared to live on porridge and water, thinking deep thoughts, walking long walks, writing poetry, providing us with moral and spiritual guidance. If only the general public had known about Annette and his daughter in France. . .

Wordsworth died at Rydal on 23 April 1850, Shakespeare's and St George's day. He had celebrated his eightieth birthday a couple of weeks earlier. Just before his passing, his wife Mary went into his room and told him that he was going to meet Dora, his beloved daughter who had died in 1847, aged forty-three.

Wordsworth's death came at midday precisely. Those who were there remembered the cuckoo clock in the hall striking the hour twelve times.

WORDSWORTH'S GRASMERE HOUSES

Dove Cottage is the Wordsworth shrine and the main attraction for tourists and scholars alike. It has come to symbolise Wordsworth's philosophy of 'plain living and high thinking'. He lived longer at Rydal Mount, but by that time he was past his best as a poet. It was at Dove Cottage that his greatest works were written. He moved in at Christmastime 1799, with Dorothy. Three of his children with Mary Hutchinson were born here. He was also joined by Sara Hutchinson, his wife's sister. Add to that a frequent flow of friends staying at this tiny, seven-roomed house and things became pretty crowded.

A postcard of Dove Cottage, Grasmere, once the home of William and Dorothy Wordsworth.

229ª DOVE COTTAGE GRASMERE
(ABRAHAMS' SERIES)

Dove Cottage is much as it was in Wordsworth's day and is very lovingly cared for. The garden has been restored and even the old summerhouse rebuilt. Except during the height of summer, log fires are usually kept burning in the grates and visitors are offered a chatty and well-informed guided tour. Inside, most of the furniture is Wordsworth's and the general aim is to keep it the way it was when he lived there; the only jarring note are a few items which belonged to Wordsworth later in life, but Dove Cottage got them first and rivalry between the Wordsworth places can be fierce.

The excellent Wordsworth Museum is next to the cottage. Best to go there first to mug up on his life before doing Dove Cottage, then you will get more out of it. The Jerwood Centre is next door, where the scholars work, though they also have events. The Wordsworth Trust is now a little industry on its own, though they hate anyone saying that they also own a nice tea room and the guest house How Foot Lodge.

Wordsworth had two other homes in Grasmere, neither of which is open to the public. Allan Bank, where he moved in 1808, is a large house, easily seen from down by the lake, as it is above the village, directly under Helm Crag. Quite a nice old house, with magnificent views over Grasmere. It is owned by the National Trust, but rented privately. It used to be white, but was repainted buff for Ken Russell's Coleridge film, *Clouds of Glory*.

The second house is the Old Parsonage, opposite St Oswald's Church. Wordsworth moved there in 1811, because the chimneys at Allan Bank smoked too much and he fell out with the landlord. It was at the parsonage that two of the Wordsworth children died – Thomas and Catherine, aged six and four – so in 1813 they decided to quit Grasmere Vale altogether and moved to Rydal.

But Grasmere still seethes with the Wordsworths. William, Mary and Dorothy are buried in the churchyard, and they also left some of their 'pet' names on the surrounding landscape. On the road above Town End, walking towards White Moss, there is a field gate that Wordsworth used to call the 'wishing gate'. Now it is somewhat unromantically covered in barbed wire.

Behind the Swan Inn, at the foot of Dunmail, is Greenhead Ghyll – the setting for Wordsworth's poem 'Michael'. Down in the village there is the Wordsworth Hotel, emblazoned with a facsimile of his signature and featuring various horrors such as the Dove and Olive Branch Bar (remembering Dove Cottage's former name), the Prelude Suite, etc. The hotel has no connection of any sort with Wordsworth. The same might be said of the portrait – supposedly of the poet – which hangs in the entrance hall. The whirring noise you can sometimes hear in Grasmere churchyard is Wordsworth spinning.

'A GERMAN' MEETS MR WORDSWORTH

In 1818, Wordsworth and Southey were doorstepped by a young German fan called Philip Kempferhausen. Here he describes his meeting with Wordsworth:

> On issuing from the noble groves in which Rydal Hall is 'bosomed high', I found myself close to the dwelling of the poet, Wordsworth, and resolved to introduce myself to him, on the strength of my letter from his illustrious brother bard. An aversion to intrude on the privacy of a great poet, intent on his lofty meditations, had hitherto deterred me from making myself known to him – but so bright and happy a spirit now lay in the beauty of the morning round his simple mansion that I entered the gate with something of the glad assurance of an ancient friendship.
>
> I soon entered the house, and was shewn into the parlour, where Mr Wordsworth and his family were assembled to breakfast. The name of Southey acted like a talisman in my favour, and I also found that my name was not unknown to the family as that of a foreigner resident in Ambleside. Their kind and affable reception of me soon relieved me from any temporary embarrassment, and when I told the circuit I had made, they seemed pleased that a foreigner should feel so enthusiastically the beauties of their country. I soon found that even the ladies well knew every step that I had taken,

and the mountains and cliffs I had just traversed. Our conversation became every moment more kind and animated, and the room was filled with gentle voices and bright smiles. I know not how to describe to you the great poet himself. There seemed to me, in his first appearance, something grave almost to austerity. . . There was not visible about him the same easy and disengaged air that so immediately charmed me in Southey – his mind seemed to require an effort to awaken itself thoroughly from some brooding train of thought, and his manner, as I felt at least, at first reluctantly relaxed into blandness and urbanity. . . The solemnity of his manner was rendered more striking by the mild simplicity of his wife, and the affectionate earnestness of his sister.. . .

The features of Wordsworth's face are strong and high, almost harsh and severe – and his eyes have, when he is silent, a dim, thoughtful, I had nearly said melancholy, expression – so that when a smile takes possession of his countenance, it is indeed the most powerful smile I ever saw. . . Smiles are, assuredly, not the abiding light on that grand countenance. . . His brow is very lofty – and his dark brown hair seems worn away, as it were, by thought, so thinly is it spread over his temples. The colour of his face is almost sallow; but it is not the sallowness of confinement or ill health, it speaks rather of the rude and boisterous greeting of the mountain weather.

After breakfast I accompanied Mr Wordsworth and his family to Grasmere Church, distant about two miles from Rydal Mount; and as we walked along, it was delightful to observe with what mingled respect and familiarity our group was saluted by all the peasants. I have not been able to observe any love of poetry among the lower orders of the people here, as in many parts of our own Germany; but the influence of a great man's character is felt in his neighbourhood, even by those who are either wholly ignorant, or but imperfectly aware of its nature.

When he speaks most earnestly, it may almost be said that he soliloquises; for he seems to obey strong internal impulses of thought and the presence of the person to whom he speaks serves merely to give his eloquence something of a didactic character.

I only recently discovered that I have Kempferhausen's letters, which were originally written to his brother in Germany and printed in *Blackwood's Magazine* in 1819. My copy of them was reprinted in a little booklet, *Letters From the Lakes*, by an Ambleside printer in 1888. I found them fascinating – and very amusing, especially now that I know who *really* wrote them. (Hurry to pages 212–13 to find out.)

THE PROBLEM WITH WORDSWORTH'S LEGS

Perhaps the sharpest description of Wordsworth was written by Thomas De Quincey (see pages 206–7), who knew him very well until they fell out.

He was, upon the whole, not a well-made man. His legs were pointedly condemned by all female connoisseurs in legs; not that they were bad in any way which would force itself upon your notice – there was no absolute deformity about them; and undoubtedly they had been serviceable legs beyond the average standard of human requisition; for calculate upon good data, that with these identical legs Wordsworth must have traversed a distance of 175,000–180,000 English miles – a mode of exercise which to him stood in the stead of alcohol and other stimulants; to which indeed he was indebted for a life of unclouded happiness and we for much of what is ex-cellent in his writings. But, useful as they have proved themselves, Wordsworth's legs were certainly not ornamental; and it was a pity, as I agreed with a lady in thinking, that he had not another pair for evening dress parties – when no boots lend their friendly aid to mask imperfections from the eyes of female rigorists.

De Quincey was fascinated by Wordsworth's marriage, as many were, and just could not imagine him ever being madly in love with a woman.

> I could not conceive of Wordsworth as submitting his faculties to the humilities and devotions of courtship. That self-surrender seemed a mere impossibility. Wordsworth, I take it upon myself to say, had not the feelings within him which makes the total devotion to a woman possible. There never lived a woman he would not have lectured and admonished under circumstances that would seem to require it; nor would he have conversed with her in any mood whatever without wearing an air of mild condescension. Wordsworth, being so, never could in any emphatic sense, have been a lover.

If only De Quincey had known about Annette. Goodness, he would have been surprised, amazed, shocked – and surely also amused and delighted. . .

WORDSWORTH'S LAST HOME

Rydal Mount was William's final home, until his death in 1850. In his own lifetime, it became a poetical shrine to his fans – he would sometimes receive as many as a hundred visitors a day, flocking to the gate just in the hope of a glimpse of the great man. After he became Poet Laureate he would issue great pronouncements on the purpose and structure of poetry. (Wordsworth has the distinction of having been a Poet Laureate who never wrote a line of official verse.)

Rydal Mount is a somewhat grander house than the Wordsworths' previous homes (see pages 192–4), and William and Dorothy both thought they had gone up in the world. Originally a sixteenth-century farmhouse, the house is still owned by a descendant of William's. Rather unimpressive from the outside, it is set in beautiful grounds – originally landscaped by William – and contains a lot of his furniture, manuscripts and possessions. When William died, most of his effects were sold off and bought by local people.

But over the years, they have gradually been returned to their former homes. The cuckoo clock that now hangs in Dove Cottage was once at Rydal Mount and its ticking used to soothe him to sleep.

At the bottom of the lane to Rydal Mount, just behind the church, is an area of land now owned by the National Trust and called Dora's Field. This has nothing to do with the daffodils of William's poem, as some visitors assume, confusing Dora with Dorothy. This was a field given by Wordsworth to his beloved daughter Dora, who died in 1847 aged 43. The real site for those notorious daffodils is on the west shore of Ullswater, in Gowbarrow Park (see page 56).

SAMUEL TAYLOR COLERIDGE (1772–1834)

Coleridge was born in Ottery St Mary in Devon in 1772, the tenth child of the vicar of Ottery who died when Samuel was seven. Coleridge was clearly very bright and gifted, something of a child prodigy. He went to school at Christ's Hospital, where he became a friend of Charles Lamb, and won a scholarship worth £67 a year to Jesus College, Cambridge, which provided him with enough money to indulge himself on alcohol and prostitutes while preaching sedition and revolution to students and staff. When his debts mounted up, he ran away and enlisted as a soldier in the Light Dragoons, calling himself Silas Tomkyn Comberbache, choosing the name to match the initials on his underwear. His brother eventually tracked him down, got him out of the army on the excuse that he was insane and paid his debts, and then he returned to Cambridge, though he never did graduate.

In 1794, while on a walking tour that took him to Oxford, he had a chance meeting with Robert Southey, then a student at Balliol. Together they set off on a lecture tour in Bristol, giving public talks on politics and theology. They hatched a scheme in which twelve young men of similar background and inclination, who all believed England was reactionary and corrupt, would go off to the New World with twelve suitable young women and found their own utopian community. The young women would, of course, be doing all

Samuel Taylor Coleridge (1772–1834).

Rydal Mount, just outside of Ambleside, is another of Wordsworth's former homes.

Rydal Mount, Wordsworth's Home.

Abraham's Series No. 326.   Keswick.

the cooking and cleaning while the men talked and debated and put the world to rights. The scheme was called Pantisocracy and they decided upon a settlement on the banks of the River Susquehanna, which none of them had been to or could properly locate, but they liked the mellifluous sound of it. Included in the plan were three sisters called Fricker. It all collapsed in the end and no one went anywhere, but Coleridge married one of the sisters, Sarah, while Southey married another, Edith.

It was in 1795, in Somerset, that Coleridge met Wordsworth and his sister Dorothy, and the two men started writing and publishing poetry together. Coleridge lived in a cottage in the village of Nether Stowey, where he wrote the poems *The Rime of the Ancient Mariner* and *Kubla Khan*, the first of which was the star turn of *Lyrical Ballads*, the volume of poetry he published with Wordsworth in 1798.

As soon as the Wordsworths were installed in Dove Cottage in 1800, Coleridge moved up to Greta Hall, in Keswick, just to be near them. (Southey and his wife would follow in 1803.) Coleridge would walk over to Dove Cottage for the evening, often via Helvellyn. He was a notable walker; in 1802 he ascended Scafell and described the experience in a letter (see page 87).

His regular visits to the Wordsworths were partly inspired by his passion for Sara Hutchinson, William's sister-in-law, which went on for around ten years, leading Coleridge to abandon his own family (leaving the Southeys to look after his wife and children at Greta Hall), take to drugs as well as alcohol and disappear on mad expeditions in Europe, before returning to sponge off the Wordsworths or other benefactors who had always admired his brilliance. For a while he had a job as acting secretary to the governor of Malta.

He continued to write poems and essays, to lecture and translate, but with little financial success. In 1816, by now addicted to opium and in a depressed state, Coleridge moved to Highgate – then a village just north of London – as a house guest of Dr James Gilman. It was there that he managed to complete his major prose work, *Biographia Literatia*. He lived for eighteen years with Dr Gilman, who managed to break him of his opium habit, but

Southey refused to have him back at Greta Hall. Coleridge died in Highgate in 1834, aged sixty-one. His daughter Sara, a literary figure in her own right, edited a collection of her father's works.

ROBERT SOUTHEY (1774–1843)

Southey was born in Bristol where his father was a linen draper. He went to Westminster School where he was expelled for writing an article called 'The Flagellant', condemning the practice of flogging. An uncle came to his rescue and provided the funds for him to go up to Oxford. All three of our Lakes Poets – Wordsworth, Coleridge and Southey – in their early, struggling, revolutionary but artistic younger days, always seemed to find either rich relations or wealthy patrons to support them when funds were low and they needed time spare to devote themselves to their literary pursuits.

Southey also moved around a lot in his early years: he went to Portugal to stay with relations, and also to Dublin, before settling down to a literary and domestic life at Greta Hall near Keswick, home also to Samuel and Sarah Coleridge. When Coleridge did a runner in 1804, Southey supported Sarah Coleridge and her children, and would do so for the rest of his life, working sometimes round the clock on books, novels, poems and journalism. He was considered one of the best reviewers and political writers of his age; at the height of his fame he could command £100 for an article in the *Spectator*, the *Morning Post* or the *Edinburgh Review* – which is roughly the same as many writers get today from similar publications. If they are lucky. Southey also wrote many works of non-fiction, including a biography of Horatio Nelson and the first history of Brazil, a country to which he had never been. The careers of both Wordsworth and Southey illustrate how it is possible to manage a professional and successful writing life despite living 300 miles from London in the back of beyond – and without phones or email.

Most of Southey's hundreds of poems have been long forgotten, though until recent decades most schoolchildren learned his poem 'The Cataract of Lodore', about Lodore Falls above Derwentwater, having it pointed out to

Robert Southey (1774–1843).

them how the words themselves seemed to tumble and fall (see page 117). Southey was also responsible for the original version of *The Three Bears*, a story he wrote for children, though many people today probably assume it was a folk tale, handed down through the generations, which no one actually wrote. In 1813 he was made Poet Laureate after his friend Walter Scott had turned it down. It gave some extra status and a small sum of money to help with his large extended family.

That same year, Southey received a letter from Charlotte Brontë, seeking his advice on some of her poems. He wrote back praising her talents, but also discouraging her from writing professionally. He said: 'Literature cannot be the business of a woman's life.' Years later, Brontë remarked to a friend that the letter was 'kind and admirable; a little stringent, but it did me good'.

Southey's wife Edith died in 1837, but after two years of depression and decline he got married again, to a writer and poet called Caroline Bowles, with whom he had been in correspondence for some time. The Wordsworths and other friends did not approve, which greatly upset him.

When Southey died in 1843, Wordsworth was not invited to the funeral, but he turned up all the same and wrote the words for an elaborate memorial inside the church at Crosthwaite, Keswick. The memorial was paid for by the government of Brazil, as thanks for his history of their country. Wordsworth then took over as Poet Laureate.

The correct pronunciation of Southey, so we are led to believe by a mocking poem written by Lord Byron, should sound like 'mouthy'. That, anyway, was the word with which he chose to rhyme Southey. So presumably it was spoken as 'South-ee'.

In 1818 Southey, like Wordsworth (see page 195), was doorstepped by a young 'German' named Philip Kempferhausen:

My first, and indeed only, interview with Mr Southey was purely accidental. I had strolled into a nursery garden, close to the small town of Keswick, and found myself at the door of a gentleman's house, on whose privacy I felt that I might seem to the inmates to have somewhat rudely intruded. On retiring from the front of the mansion, I met a gentleman, to whom I apologised for my seeming intrusion; and being received with a singular courtesy, I found myself sitting in an elegant little parlour, with my unknown host, a lady, who I saw was his wife, and two very beautiful children. . . Mr Southey allowed me, with frank and unaffected good nature, to express my sense of the honour I enjoyed, and then changed the conversation with some lively remarks on the weather, which was oppressively hot; and, unless I am greatly mistaken, he uttered two of those little witticisms called puns. There was indeed something short and epigrammatic in his talk, and I felt rather puzzled how to take my share in the conversation; for I could not think of shewing off as a facetious person before a great poet. . . I soon felt myself perfectly at ease; for there was no affectation in this lively and happy carelessness of mind, evidently unbending itself with pleasure in the bosom of a beautiful family, from those severe and higher studies which have raised his name among the immortals; and e'er an hour elapsed, I was absolutely exchanging repartees with the poet; and on one occasion I thought his smile admitted that I had said a tolerably good thing. During all this time I was, in spite of myself, acting in the character of a well-intentioned spy.

THOMAS DE QUINCEY (1785–1859)

De Quincey was born in Manchester, the son of a prosperous linen manufacturer, Thomas Quincey, who died when he was seven. (Wordsworth and Southey, of course, also lost parents when they were young.) He went for a while to Manchester Grammar School as a boarder, then dropped out, wandered around Wales for six months and then went to London where he lived in Soho with a sixteen-year-old prostitute. Or so he maintained. He was rescued from Soho by his guardian, who got him into Oxford.

As a schoolboy, De Quincey read *Lyrical Ballads* and was overwhelmed. When he wrote to Wordsworth in 1803 to tell him so – one of the great man's first ever fan letters – Wordsworth invited him to visit. De Quincey made it as far as Coniston, stayed the night in an inn, but was then overcome by nerves and shyness and decided to return to Oxford.

After leaving Oxford – where he first began to use opium – he studied for the bar at the Inner Temple for a while and then gave up, deciding he was going to try to make a living for himself as a writer. By now he had added the 'De' to his name, augmenting the rather common-or-garden-sounding 'Thomas Quincey', the name he'd had from birth.

In 1807 he managed to get himself introduced to Coleridge in the West Country and then followed him up to the Lake District. When Coleridge fell on hard financial times, De Quincey anonymously advanced him £300, saying it was from 'a young man of fortune who admired his talents'.

He finally met the Wordsworths, who were greatly taken by this clever and amusing young man. De Quincey eventually took over Dove Cottage when the Wordsworths moved out and was the tenant for the next twenty-five years, though he did not always live there full-time. Dorothy made him some curtains, and was amazed at the huge quantity of books he owned.

He upset the Wordsworths when, not long after he had moved in, he knocked down the summerhouse and cut down the orchard to let more light into the cottage. Dorothy refused to speak to him after that. The Wordsworths further snubbed him when he began an affair with a local farmer's daughter, Margaret Simpson, whom he eventually married in 1817 and who bore him eight children.

In 1818 De Quincey became the second editor of the *Westmorland Gazette*, thanks to the patronage of the Lowthers, but he got the sack for not going to the office – which sounds like a reasonable sacking offence. Thereafter he made a precarious living by writing for various magazines and by translating German authors into English. His wanderings took him to Edinburgh, where he contributed reviews, articles and stories to *Blackwood's* and *Tait's* magazines.

Thomas De Quincey (1785–1859).

De Quincey struggled throughout his life with money worries and various physical ailments, and it was because of the latter that he resorted increasingly to opium. A literary by-product of his addiction was the book for which he was, and is, best known, *Confessions of an English Opium-Eater*, published in 1821 in the *London Magazine*. De Quincey also wrote a wonderful book of gossip and memories of the Lake Poets, called simply *Recollections of the Lake Poets*. He died in Edinburgh in 1859.

Of all the so-called Lake Poets – lumping De Quincey with Wordsworth, Coleridge and Southey – Thomas De Quincey's prose is the most enjoyable and interesting to read today, and in some ways has hardly dated, being waspish, wicked and amusing. He was a sharp observer of Wordsworth, who fancied himself every winter as an ice skater on the frozen lakes, but according to De Quincey he 'sprawled like a cow dancing a cotillion'.

FIVE LITERARY VISITORS

The Scottish poet and novelist Walter Scott (1771–1832) was a frequent visitor to the Lakes and a friend of the Lake Poets. He first came as a guest of Wordsworth and stayed with him at Dove Cottage. He was so put off by the meals (too much 'plain living' for his tastes) that he used to climb out of his bedroom window every morning and go to the Swan Inn in the village for a proper breakfast, before returning and getting back into bed as if nothing had happened. He used Castle Rock in St John's in the Vale as the setting for his narrative poem, *The Bridal of Triermain*.

*

The writer and essayist William Hazlitt (1778–1830) visited Southey at Greta Hall, but left in a rush, pursued by villagers, having got himself rather too involved with one of the local girls.

*

The poet Percy Bysshe Shelley (1792–1822) eloped to Scotland with Harriet Westbrook, a sixteen-year-old schoolgirl. He lived in Keswick in 1811–12, visiting the Southeys.

*

Felicia Hemans (1793–1835), author of the poem 'Casabianca' (which opens with the oft-quoted words 'The boy stood on the burning deck'), is not very famous today, but she was well known in her day, and became a popular poet from a very young age (Shelley wrote her a fan letter when she was just fifteen). She lived for a while at a house called the Dove Nest in Ambleside and became a friend of the Wordsworths.

*

The poet John Keats (1795–1821) came to the area in 1818. He visited Rydal Mount to see Wordsworth and climbed up to the waterfalls at Stock Ghyll in Ambleside. He also climbed Skiddaw and described Castlerigg Stone Circle in his poem 'Hyperion' as:

Scarce images of life, one here, one there,
Lay vast and edgeways; like a dismal cirque
Of Druid stones, upon a forlorn moor. . .

A portrait of Walter Scott by William Allan, c. 1844.

6

Later Literary and Artistic Folk

*Summer brought a succession of visitors – very
agreeable, but rather too many for my strength
and repose. I began to find what are the liabilities
of Lake residents in regard to tourists.*

HARRIET MARTINEAU, 1870S

WILLIAM WORDSWORTH AND HIS FELLOW LAKE POETS attracted many other poets and writers to the area, and over the decades since a steady stream of artists of one kind or another have come to live in Lakeland.

JOHN WILSON (CHRISTOPHER NORTH) (1785–1854)

John Wilson was one of Lakeland's greatest characters, a giant of a man, over six feet and sixteen stone, who enjoyed sailing, dancing, fishing, boxing, Cumberland and Westmorland wrestling, cock fighting (even in his own drawing room) and also loved pranks, literary and otherwise.

He was born in Paisley where his father was a wealthy gauze manufacturer. He went to Glasgow University and then Oxford, where he was a contemporary of little weedy Thomas De Quincey, though they never met. Wilson was an Oxford legend for his japes, physical presence and prowess. As so many young men did, he wrote a fan letter to Wordsworth in 1802, and got a nice reply back.

On leaving Oxford – his father having died and left him £50,000 – he bought a large estate at Elleray, near Orrest Head on Windermere, and lived there for the next ten years. He wrote many books under the name of Christopher North, creating a fanciful persona for himself, with exaggerated and amusing accounts of his exploits, as well as novels, journalism and essays. He got to know the Wordsworths and all the quality folk of the time, giving parties, organising regattas on Windermere, striding around the county, mixing with all sorts and conditions. He had his own fleet of sailing ships and called himself the Lord High Admiral of Windermere.

He loved Lakeland, and wrote about it copiously and enthusiastically, and it was something he had written that first made Harriet Martineau (see below) get up off her sick bed and come to Lakeland.

He eventually pushed his luck with the Wordsworths a bit too far, mocking them behind their back, and it was he who was responsible for the pretend letters from the German student, Philip Kempferhausen (see page 195). Not

PREVIOUS SPREAD
Ambleside seen from the
shoulder of Loughrigg.

only did he satirise Wordsworth and the over-the-top Lakeland lovers, he also revealed some details that had come from his personal friendship with the Wordsworths. Even worse, as the German student was assumed to be real, the letters encouraged other students to doorstep Wordsworth. At one time it was suspected that De Quincey was behind the jape, but now all the academics – such as the late Robert Woof of Dove Cottage – have decided it was Wilson.

Eventually Wilson's money ran out and he moved to Edinburgh where he got himself elected Professor of Moral Philosophy, his lectures being highly popular. Almost all his works have been forgotten today, but his name and character live on, thanks to the many references to him in the writings of his contemporaries, who loved his gaiety, his enthusiasm and his wit – as long as they were not on the receiving end, of course.

HARRIET MARTINEAU (1802–76)

Harriet Martineau was an all-round literary figure, early feminist, traveller and eccentric who built the Knoll at Ambleside, and lived there for thirty years. She wrote *A Complete Guide to the English Lakes* (but didn't give star ratings to anything). She was born in Norwich, was educated at a Unitarian college and got engaged to a fellow Unitarian student, but he died within a year of brain fever. Harriet never did get married. When the family money ran out she went up to London to make a living as a writer, contributing to all the major magazines, such as Charles Dickens's *Household Words*, and also wrote many books. She went off to the United States for two years and came back a fervent opponent of the slave trade. She wrote a colourful account of her experiences in the US, which sold well. The indomitable Harriet also visited Egypt and Palestine and got another book out of it.

She came to Ambleside in 1845, partly for her health, loving the open air, and partly attracted by Wordsworth and co. They were a little bit suspicious of this strident feminist and campaigner at first, but they made her welcome.

She became a friend of Wordsworth and he planted a tree in her garden at the Knoll. She took part in lots of local campaigns and activities and generally threw herself into Lakeland life. Her visitors at various times included Charlotte Brontë, George Eliot and Matthew Arnold.

✻

Harriet Martineau wrote a sparky description of life in Ambleside in the 1870s in her autobiography. In some ways, not a lot has changed...

> Summer brought a succession of visitors – very agreeable, but rather too many for my strength and repose. I began to find what are the liabilities of Lake residents in regard to tourists. There is quite wear and tear enough in receiving those whom one wishes to see; one's invited guests or those introduced by one's invited friends. But these are fewer than the unscrupulous strangers who intrude themselves with compliments, requests for autographs, or without any pretence whatever. Every summer they come and stare in at the windows while we are at dinner, hide behind shrubs or the corner of the house, plant themselves in the yards behind or the field before; are staring up at one's window when one gets up in the morning, gather handfuls of flowers in the garden, stop or follow us in the road, and report us to the newspapers. I soon found that I must pay a serious tax for living in my paradise: I must, like many of my neighbours, go away in 'the tourist season'. My practice has since been to let my house for the months of July, August and September – or for the two latter at least, and go to the sea or some country place where I could be quiet.
>
> The constitution of our town suffers six months of the year from fever and the other six from collapse. In the summertime our inns are filled to bursting; our private houses broken into by parties desperate after lodgings; the prices of every thing are quadrupled; our best meat, our thickest cream, our freshest fish, are reserved for

Harriet Martineau (1802–76).

strangers; our letters, delivered three hours after time, have been opened and read by banditti assuming our own title; ladies of quality, loaded with tracts, fusillade us; savage and bearded foreigners harass us with brazen wind instruments; coaches run frantically towards us from every point of the compass; a great steam-monster ploughs our lake and disgorges multitudes upon the pier, the excursion-trains bring thousands of curious vulgar, who mistake us for the author-ess next door and compel us to forge her autograph; the donkeys in our streets increase and multiply a hundred-fold, tottering under the weight of enormous females visiting our waterfalls from morn to eve; our hills are darkened by swarms of tourists; we are ruth-lessly eyed by painters and brought into foregrounds and backgrounds as 'warm tints' or 'bits of repose'; our lawns are picnicked upon by twenty at a time and our trees branded with initial letters; creatures with introductions come to us and can't be got away; we have to lionise poor, stupid and ill-looking people for weeks without past, present or future recompense. The fever lasts from May until October.

Harriet Martineau, *Autobiography,* 1877

JAMES SPEDDING (1808–81)

The Spedding family of Mirehouse (see page 61), on the shores of Bas-senthwaite, four miles north of Keswick, were not national literary figures in the sense of producing much notable literature themselves, but they were awfully well connected.

James Spedding, born in 1808 at Mirehouse and educated at Trinity College Cambridge, was a noted literary figure of the nineteenth century, the author of a multi-volume biography of Francis Bacon. One of his more illustrious visitors at Mirehouse was Alfred Tennyson, who stayed there while working on his version of the Arthurian legend. He used Bassenthwaite in his description of Arthur's death – it was on this lake that the black barge bore away King Arthur's body in *Idylls of the King.*

Thomas Carlyle was a frequent visitor to Mirehouse, too. He said that it was 'beautiful and so were the ways of it. . . not to speak of Skiddaw and the finest mountains on earth'. Not only was James Spedding the host for some of the literary notables of his day, his family also had literary connections. His father, John, spent six years in the same class as Wordsworth at Hawkshead Grammar School.

James Spedding died in London in 1881, from injuries received when he was knocked down by a hansom cab.

*

The Spedding family still live at Mirehouse. In 2009 John Spedding produced a pretty booklet called *An Uncommonplace Book*, a collection of nineteenth-century wit and letters, which he'd dug out from his family archives – from diaries, commonplace books, journals and children's writings. The book includes some of the stories, jokes and riddles that well-bred nineteenth-century literary types told each other round the fireplace, and also some of the letters from the famous people who stayed at Mirehouse, such as Alfred Tennyson, Thomas Carlyle and Edward Fitzgerald.

Some of the riddles, now at least 150 years old, are just as funny today – or unfunny and pathetic, depending on how much Christmas cheer you have knocked back:

Q: Why is a man about to put his father into a sack like a traveller journeying to an Eastern city?
A: Because he is going to Baghdad.

Q: If a man bites a bit off the top of your nose, what does the law command you to do?
A: Keep the piece.

Possibly of more lasting literary interest is a thank-you letter from Thomas Carlyle to James's elder brother Thomas Spedding, written on 19 October 1847. Carlyle has had a holiday at Mirehouse and is now back home in Chelsea, having caught the train from Windermere.

I had a beautiful drive that Tuesday morning; the weather, the scene, the equipage altogether agreeable. The swift brooks, clear as liquid diamonds, sang their best song for me, the last I was to hear of the brooks for a twelvemonth to come: Helvellyn and the everlasting hills, Grasmere steeple and the transitory villages and chapels; things seen for the first time, and things seen long years ago, preached equally a mild and wholesome sermon for me. In silence, too, and no reply needed – no falsity, except one volunteered it! I shall long remember that mild solitary morning, and its doctrines and melodies. Once swallowed into the belly of the rail-train, there was of course nothing more to be said or thought, nine hours of tempestuous deafening nightmare, like hours of Jonah in the whale's belly, I support, and one was flung out in Euston Square, glad to have escaped but stupefied for a week to come. Absolutely I think ether must come in vogue, if man persists in that mode of travelling. To man who has still his sense left, the operation is too painful. At Chelsea I found my wife better than I had expected and nothing at all gone wrong in my absence; my wife, I rather judge, continues to amend: I am charged with kind remembrances to Mrs Spedding and from her brother, and thanks for your goodness to me.

At Windermere Station, while the tumult of packing went on, a foolish lady with noisy foolish children in the carriage beside us, pointed out to one of them a figure on the platform as 'Mr Coleridge, whom you saw this morning, my dawlings!' The figure, hoary, small and in clothes too small for it; with a switch in its hand, an almost idiotic stereotype simper on its face; apparently taking leave of some female Lakers, instantly arrested all my attention: poor Hartley Coleridge himself, and no mistake. . .

Thomas Carlyle to Thomas Spedding, 19 October 1847,
from An Uncommonplace Book, John Spedding, 2009

Hartley Coleridge was Samuel Taylor Coleridge's son, always known as Li'l Hartley. When Hartley was young he was greatly loved by the Wordsworths. He later went to Oxford and became a minor literary figure, but by 1847 he was a rather sad figure, living at Nab Cottage beside Rydal Water and drinking too much.

CHARLOTTE BRONTË (1816–55)

Charlotte Brontë first visited the Lakes in August 1850 but had been brought up on Wordsworth and Coleridge and knew all about the wonders of the Lakeland landscape. When she was younger, she had written to Southey and also to Wordsworth and Coleridge.

Her father had persuaded her to accept an invitation from Sir James Kay Shuttleworth and Lady Shuttleworth to a house known as Briery Close, which they had rented on the shores of Lake Windermere, just above the little landing stage at Low Wood. Charlotte found the countryside 'exquisitely beautiful'. She wrote in her diary: 'The Lake Country is a glorious region, of which I had only seen the similitude in dreams, waking or sleeping.'

But alas, now that Charlotte had finally made it to Lakeland, all the poets she was interested in had passed away: Southey had been dead for seven years, Hartley Coleridge had died in 1849 and Wordsworth in April 1850. She did, however, get to meet the novelist Elizabeth Gaskell.

Sir James Kay Shuttleworth had got to know Mrs Gaskell in Manchester, before he met Charlotte Brontë, and he now invited the author of *Mary Barton* to meet the writer of *Jane Eyre* at Briery Close. An eyewitness who was present described Charlotte Brontë as extremely nervous and shy, looking as if she would be glad if the floor would open to swallow her, while Mrs

Charlotte Brontë (1816–55).

Gaskell sat bright, cheerful and quite at ease. But the two women became firm friends. 'I like her very much; her manner is kind, candid and unassuming,' wrote Charlotte in a letter. And it was Mrs Gaskell who would write the first biography of Charlotte Brontë, published in 1857.

Later that year, in December 1850, Charlotte Brontë accepted an invitation to stay for a few days with Harriet Martineau. According to Mrs Ellis Chadwick in her 1895 book *In the Footsteps of the Brontës*, Harriet traipsed round the lanes and paths of Ambleside in her stout boots and skirt with Charlotte trailing behind, not being much of a walker and being rather delicate. Charlotte noticed how Miss Martineau seemed to rule Ambleside like an autocrat. They did not have much in common, except for both being writers, but Charlotte admired Harriet for her strength and also for her modesty about her writings.

JOHN RUSKIN (1819–1900)

John Ruskin, art critic, writer, philosopher and champion of many social causes, first came to the Lakes as a young boy in 1824, then again in 1826, 1830, 1837 and 1838. Like many well-born children of the upper middle classes, he was taken on family trips to Lakeland.

Ruskin was born in Bloomsbury, the son of doting Scottish parents (especially his mother). His father was a wealthy wine merchant, connected with the sherry- importing firm of Domecq – until recently still a well-known name in the drinks business. Ruskin went up to Christ Church, Oxford, accompanied by his mother who took lodgings nearby. He was a great traveller, often with his parents, and wrote diaries and poems about his travels. In response to an attack on J. M. W. Turner in *Blackwood's Magazine*, he wrote a stout defence, which turned him into the champion of Turner and other artists. He wrote many books and essays about art and became the first Slade Professor of Fine Art at Oxford.

In 1848 he married Euphemia 'Effie' Chalmers Gray, the twenty-year-old daughter of family friends who lived in Perth in Scotland. When divorce followed six years later, it was the talk of Victorian London. Effie maintained that Ruskin was incurably impotent and the marriage had never been consummated. He alleged that there was something wrong with her, a 'physical blemish', which made sexual intercourse impossible. This is thought to have been her pubic hair, which Ruskin did know existed but which had horrified him. It was all blamed on his over-coddling mother, of course. Effie then married the artist Sir John Everett Millais and had several children. The whole marriage saga provided excellent copy for diarists and writers of the time – and later for film-makers.

It was in 1871, at the age of fifty-two, having inherited his father's estate, that Ruskin decided to settle in Lakeland. He bought Brantwood on the eastern side of Coniston Water for £1,500, without even first seeing the place. 'Any place opposite Coniston Old Man must be beautiful,' he said. In the event, he got 'a mere shed of rotten timbers and loose stone', but Ruskin transformed it into a beautiful home and stocked it with art treasures (particularly the paintings of Turner). He lived there for the last thirty years of his life.

Today, Brantwood is open to the public (which was Ruskin's original wish) and has been transformed into an excellent museum and country house. As a tourist attraction it now rivals the other Lake District big guns – Dove Cottage, Hill Top and Rydal Mount. Brantwood contains many of Ruskin's paintings and possessions. Look out for the Ruskin-designed wallpaper in the downstairs rooms. It's nice to see the political message of his writings coming across in a video of his life and work, normally shown in one of the downstairs rooms. Ruskin fought hard against the worst aspects of Victorian society and values, and Brantwood's fifteen-acre garden is kept in his spirit (he abhorred 'fashionable' gardens), with the 'Professor's Garden' restored following Ruskin's own description of the layout. The steam yacht *Gondola* (see page 58–60) calls regularly at Brantwood's jetty.

There is a Ruskin Museum in Coniston village and a monument to him at Friar's Crag on Derwentwater that bears the following words of his: 'The

A postcard of John Ruskin at Brantwood.

John Ruskin at Brantwood

Abrahams' Series, Keswick.

first thing I remember as an event in life was being taken by my nurse to the brow at Friar's Crag on Derwentwater.' This was when he was five, on his first Lakeland tour.

＊

The diary John Ruskin kept of his 1830 tour of Lakeland, when he was just eleven years old, was edited by an American Ruskin scholar and published in 1990. On this tour he was accompanied by his parents and a nurse. The diary shows his precocious nature – it tells us that the mountains were 'extremely sublime' – but also his child's eye: in Kendal they visit the castle, 'which looks very well from the town, but is a disagreeable nettly place when you are in it'. Young Ruskin also managed to snoop on both Wordsworth and Southey, but didn't manage a proper conversation with the great men.

27 June, Sunday, Keswick
On Sunday we went to Crosthwaite Church, which is about a mile from the town of Keswick. We were put in a seat, that would have been a disgrace to any church, it was so dirty, but we easily put up with that as in the seat directly opposite Mr Southey sat. We saw him very nicely. He seemed extremely attentive & by what we saw of him we should think him very pious. He has a very keen eye & looks extremely like a poet. We had a very pleasant walk in the afternoon.

4 July, Sunday, Low Wood
The next morning being Sunday we went to Rydal Chapel in preference to Ambleside as we heard that Mr Wordsworth went to Rydal, which is a most beautiful little chapel built by Lady Fleming. The windows were executed with none of the modern finery but yet with great chasteness & elegance. The most beautiful little chapel we ever saw.

Brantwood, John Ruskin's house on the eastern shore of Coniston Water.

We were lucky in procuring a seat very near that of Mr Wordsworth, there being only one between it & the one we were in. We were rather disappointed in this gentleman's appearance, especially as he appeared asleep the greatest part of the time. He seemed about 60. This gentleman possesses a long face and a large nose with a moderate assortment of grey hairs and two small grey eyes with a mouth of moderate dimensions that is quite large enough to let in a sufficient quantity of beef or mutton & to let out a sufficient quantity of poetry.

5 July, Monday, Low Wood
On Monday morning shortly after breakfast we set out in a boat to visit the station about five miles from Low Wood. We had a very pleasant sail down the lake and landed on an island belonging to Mr Curwen & on which he had a house. It is the largest [island] in the lake, being about a mile long.

On leaving the station we re-entered our boat & crossed the lake to Bowness, a beautiful little village situated on the border of the lake. The village itself is much more beautiful than the bay on which it is situated, as the beach is not wanting in dead cats & dogs, & the water is dirty from the quantity of boats continually sailing about the bay & when they land ploughing up the sand at the bottom with their keels.

CANON RAWNSLEY (1851–1920)

Canon Rawnsley was a literary figure, in that he wrote a great number of books, but he was much more than that – he was a towering figure in Lakeland and national life, an indefatigable campaigner and activist. Today he is best known, and most admired, for being a co-founder of the National Trust.

I first came across his name when I was fourteen and my violin teacher entered me for the Rawnsley Prize at the Carlisle Music Festival, an honour in itself. I came fourth out of four, being rubbish on the violin. There was also some Rawnsley Shield when I was in the Boy Scouts, but I can't remember what it was for. Knots or woggles, probably. Then I grew up and forgot the name Rawnsley.

A few years ago, after writing several books about railways and Lakeland, and about Beatrix Potter and Wordsworth, in which Rawnsley kept appearing as a minor walk-on character, I tried to persuade several London publishers to let me do his biography. They all yawned, saying it must be time for lunch. No, but, he was an amazing man, I said. An unknown Victorian vicar, they said, who lived in some obscure part of the provinces? Who wants to read a book about him? So I never got it off the ground, which was a shame.

✻

Canon Rawnsley was born Hardwicke Drummond Rawnsley in Shiplake, near Henley, in 1851. His father, a vicar, was a close friend of Tennyson, and had officiated at his wedding. The young Hardwicke decided he wanted to be a poet when he grew up. On his mother's side, he was related to Sir John Franklin, the Arctic explorer and great Victorian hero, so when he wasn't dreaming about poetry he was imagining himself as a great explorer.

He went to Uppingham School, and Balliol College, Oxford, where he rowed and ran and wrote poetry. He became a friend of Ruskin, Slade Professor of Fine Art, and Benjamin Jowett, the Master of Balliol. Jowett discouraged Rawnsley's passion for poetry, saying he should settle down and 'get rid of his excitable ways'.

In 1877, he became vicar of Wray, on the western shores of Windermere. It is not quite clear why an energetic and muscular cleric was moved at such a young age to a remote rural parish, but while doing missionary work in Soho he appears to have had some sort of breakdown. Or perhaps his excitable ways had made him enemies.

He married a local girl, Edith Fletcher from Ambleside, and threw himself into every aspect of Lakeland life. He often visited Ruskin, who by then was living at Brantwood on Coniston (see page 220). He set himself the task of recording memories of local people who had known Wordsworth. In 1881, he had his own book of Lake District sonnets published – mostly soppy, some religious.

In 1882, Beatrix Potter, then aged sixteen, came to spend a long holiday in his parish when her well-off parents rented Wray Castle for the summer. He became great friends with her parents and with her, praising her little drawings and paintings, and encouraging her interest in animals and plants.

∗

Early in 1883, Rawnsley became involved in his first big campaign. There was a proposal for a railway from Buttermere to Keswick, primarily to carry slate from Honister, which he said would ruin some beautiful landscape. He wrote storming letters to the national press, organised petitions and action groups

Canon Hardwicke Rawnsley (1851–1920).

– and by April he'd had the bill thrown out. His first campaign – and his first victory. Not an easy one, because the country was in the grip of railway mania.

That year, at the annual meeting of the Wordsworth Society, presided over by Matthew Arnold, Rawnsley proposed the formation of a Lake District Defence Society. Within a year, there were 600 members (only 10 per cent of whom actually lived in the Lake District), including Tennyson, Browning and the duke of Westminster. Their first fight was against a proposed railway in Ennerdale – which was also won.

*

In 1883, the bishop of Carlisle offered Rawnsley the living of Crosthwaite, Keswick, a more important parish, more at the centre of Lakeland life (see page 126). For the next twenty-five years, Canon Rawnsley (as he became in 1893) was based in Keswick – but the whole of England was really his parish.

On a local level, he created the Keswick School of Industrial Art, which started as a series of evening classes in his parish hall, teaching local lads and lasses woodcarving, metalwork, drawing and painting. He served for many years as a Cumberland county councillor, campaigning for the poor and the homeless. He was the first president of the Cumberland Nature Club, which took children on nature walks.

His interests and campaigns expanded to a national level, and many of them now seem astoundingly modern: against pollution in streams; pro-organic farming; up with pure milk; down with white bread. Rawnsley believed that the new fashion for bleached bread was 'starving the nation, robbing it of bone for the body, enamel for the teeth and proteins for the tissue'. So active was he in this campaign that a bread manufacturer threatened libel action.

*

Rawnsley also had some fairly eccentric, not to say dopey, passions, such as bonfires. In 1887, for Queen Victoria's Jubilee, he was put in charge of Lakeland's celebratory bonfires. He led an excursion of 400 people up Skiddaw, where they were able to admire 148 different bonfires glowing all over Lakeland, which Rawnsley had organised.

In 1901, he got very steamed about a new and terrible evil – penny-in-the-slot machines at railway stations; Rawnsley was concerned that impressionable young men were being corrupted by 'indecent and degrading pictures'. He managed to have them removed from every station platform. He also wrote to chief constables in his campaign against rude picture postcards – the sort sold at Blackpool – and alerted the nation to the harm that could be done by another innovation: the cinema. He proposed the censorship of films showing sex or violence before they could be shown to children.

I have this image of him: big, bearded and burly, a hyperactive Terry Waite, forever bustling around the countryside, stirring things up. I've made up his bigness – the only book about him, written by his widow and published in 1923, doesn't give his size, or many other personal details. I know he was a good public speaker and had appalling handwriting. I sense that as he got older he grew bossier, like many do-gooders whose hearts are in the right place. He missed the London train once, leaving from Keswick, but ordered the station master to summon another for him.

In 1898, he received a letter from the archbishop of Canterbury, asking whether he would like to be bishop of Madagascar. A strange offer, and not, I suspect, from a well-wisher, but his friends and fellow campaigners persuaded him to stay. His real work was at home.

*

Rawnsley's greatest work, for which we must all be grateful, was the National Trust. The origins, for him, went back to 1885 and a local dispute concerning public footpaths along Derwentwater and over Latrigg. Two landowners had closed the paths with barriers. He wrote letters of complaint, which the landowners ignored on the grounds that no one was really interested, and that Rawnsley was one of just two or three agitators stirring things up. Rawnsley led a deputation of 400 to the home of one of the landowners, and then a public march of 2,000 along the footpath that had been closed. Next he held protest meetings in London, Oxford, Manchester, Liverpool and elsewhere. Finally, he took the campaign to court, to the Carlisle assizes, where the case was won and the footpaths kept open.

In 1893, Rawnsley was alarmed when the Lodore Falls and the island in the middle of Grasmere came up for sale. He felt that such sites should always be available to the public, yet there was no existing organisation capable of buying and caring for them. Many years earlier, Wordsworth had suggested that there should be some body to protect the Lakes. John Ruskin had mouthed much the same. But it was the bold, energetic and practical Canon Rawnsley who put these noble ideals into practice.

He contacted two other notable campaigners, with whom he had worked defending footpaths and other causes, both of them old friends: Octavia Hill and Sir Robert Hunter. The three met at the duke of Westminster's house in London for a preliminary meeting, and from this the National Trust was formed, attaining legal status in 1895. The duke was made president and Rawnsley was the first secretary, a position he held for the next twenty-five years, till his death in 1920. The first life member was Rupert Potter, Beatrix's father.

Which brings us to Rawnsley's second great achievement. Young Beatrix, at that time, was getting nowhere with her little drawings, as Rawnsley knew. After that first summer on Windermere, the Potters had visited Lakeland many times and he had remained a close friend. By 1900, she'd had ten years of rejections from publishers.

Rawnsley suggested that she write and illustrate her own book. She sat down at once and wrote a story about a rabbit called Peter. Rawnsley, by then a published author himself, drew up a list of six publishers she should try. He knew the publishing business well, so he boasted. All turned her down.

But you don't get to be a successful campaigner by giving up easily. Rawnsley suggested she publish the book herself, using her own money, doing it in black and white to keep it cheap. She printed 250 copies, price 1s 2d each, most of which she gave away. (Recently, one of these editions sold for £50,000.)

Rawnsley was still keen for Beatrix to find a proper publisher, and offered to rewrite the Peter Rabbit story himself, in his own verse. The publisher Frederick Warne finally accepted the book, but fortunately declined Rawnsley's rewrite. Their edition, in colour, came out in 1902 – and the rest is children's history.

Were they in love? If I'd done his biography, I would certainly have investigated this. Well, or suggested it. In that 1923 book, written by his second wife, Eleanor, whom he married in 1918 after the death of his first wife, there is no mention of his connection with Beatrix Potter. It is believed in the family that Eleanor was a little jealous.

BEATRIX POTTER (1866–1943)

Beatrix Potter was a Londoner, born there in 1866, but her family had connections with Lancashire cotton and she spent her holidays from the age of sixteen in the Lake District, in rented but rather grand houses, round Windermere and Derwentwater. Her parents were genteel, upper-middle-class Edwardians and she was educated at home and expected to devote her life to her parents, or to get married. She found an outlet for her artistic talents in drawing and painting 'little books for children'. Encouraged by the family's Lakeland friend Canon Rawnsley, she decided to self-publish, using her own money, and her first book, *The Tale of Peter Rabbit*, was published in 1901.

With the money she made from her twenty-four 'little' books, such as *The Tale of Jemima Puddle-Duck*, *The Tale of Mrs Tiggy-Winkle* and *The Tale of Squirrel Nutkin*, all with Lakeland settings, she bought Hill Top Farm at Near Sawrey in 1905 and then further Lakeland properties.

In 1913, she married William Heelis, a local solicitor who had handled some of her property purchases. From then on she devoted her life to her farms and to the preservation of the countryside, doing a great deal to help the work of the National Trust, thanks again to the friendship and encouragement of Canon Rawnsley.

Beatrix Potter died in 1943, and all her property – fifteen farms with their Herdwick flocks, many cottages and 4,000 acres of land – came to the National Trust. She asked that the Herdwicks, her favourite sheep, should continue to be bred, and that both farms and cottages should have reliable local tenants.

Most of the original illustrations for her books eventually came to the Trust and can now be seen in the Hawkshead Gallery.

Beatrix Heelis, as she always signed and called herself after her marriage, never actually lived in Hill Top. She kept the original seventeenth-century building for her own use, as a sort of museum to Lakeland farming life. She wrote many of her books there and sometimes was able to stay for a few nights, but that was all. Nearby Castle Cottage became her home after she married William Heelis.

On her death in 1943, Beatrix's ashes were scattered locally, somewhere in the fields around Hill Top. The precise location has never been revealed. But in 1978, while researching for my book *A Walk Around the Lakes* (published in 1979), I had an interesting encounter near Hill Top.

A MEETING WITH BEATRIX POTTER'S SHEPHERD

I left the house and was walking in the fields beside Hill Top Farm when I came across an old man standing beside an awful-smelling bonfire. He said he was burning wellingtons. We stood chatting, me being an expert on wellies and their myriad qualities, and he turned out to be an expert on Beatrix Potter. I hadn't realised there were any locals left who had worked for her, as the National Trust goes to some lengths to restrict publicity about Hill Top Farm. He said his name was Tom Storey and that for eighteen and a half years he'd worked for Mrs Heelis as a shepherd and then farm bailiff. He was aged eighty-two but looked a good twenty years younger.

Beatrix Potter at Hill Top Farm in 1905.

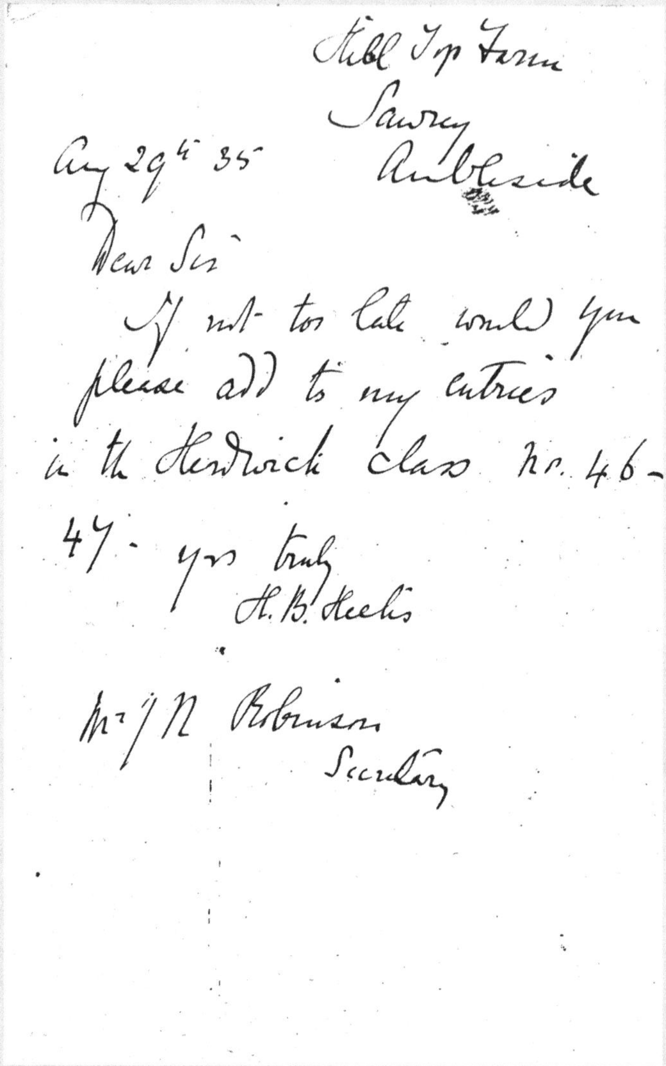

Hill Top Farm
Sawrey
Ambleside

Aug 29th 35

Dear Sir

If not too late would you
please add to my entries
in the Herdwick class no. 46 –
47 – yrs truly
H. B. Heelis

Mr J N Robinson
Secretary

In 1943, on her death, she left him £400 and instructed that, though the farm was to go to the National Trust, he should take over the tenancy. This he did, farming Hill Top Farm till he retired and then handing the tenancy over to his son. He's eternally grateful for her kindness – though, being a true Lakelander, there was no trace of sentimentality in his memories of her.

Even now, he's surprised by the success of her books. She gave his children autographed copies of *The Fairy Caravan*, the first copies from the press, which they still have. 'You can read them all in twenty minutes,' he said, turning over the ashes of the wellies. 'Yet she made all that money from them. I can't understand it.'

In the standard biography of Beatrix Potter by Margaret Lane it says her fellow farmers sought her opinion on Herdwicks at sheep fairs and that she was 'one of the shrewdest farmers in the Lake Country'. Other publications about Beatrix Potter speak equally highly about her great farming expertise.

'Just a fallacy,' said Mr Storey. 'What could she know about farming, coming out of London? She liked Herdwicks, right enough. She'd look at no other, but she could make mistakes when judging them. I could give you examples, but I don't like to. It wouldn't be fair, after all these years. I'll tell you just one. At Keswick Show one year we'd won everything and she was taking someone round. "These are the ewes we won with, aren't they, Storey?" They weren't. They were Willy Rigg's. Ours were in the next pen. . .'

'She wasn't a bad farmer, I'll say that. We had our flaps. We differed over some things, but I didn't take much notice. I just got on with it. When you've gone through it all as a boy, you just carry on.

'I told her many a time that she'd be better off having some cattle instead of all Herdwicks. She was losing some money by having just Herdwicks, and I once got very worried. "Don't you worry, Storey," she told me. "It's only a hobby."'

Despite her privileged London background, which in Storey's eyes could never make her a farmer, he said she had a plain voice and not a Kensington one, and she loved to hear the real Westmorland dialect. He was obviously

One of my Lakeland treasures: a letter from Beatrix Potter – writing under her married name H. B. Heelis – written at Hill Top to the secretary of the Loweswater Show, 1935.

CHAMPION PRIZES.

Mrs. Heelis, Castle Cottage, Sawrey, Ambleside, will give a
Silver Cup, for the best Three Tups, consisting of 1 Two-shear
(not showing more than four broad teeth), 1 shearling and 1 Lamb.
To be won three times in all by same exhibitor.
Awarded 1931 to Lord Leconfield.
1934 to Mr. W. N. Park

S. D. Stanley-Dodgson, Esq., Armaside, will give a Silver Cup
value £5 for the best Herdwick (male) in the Foregoing
classes. To be won three times in all by the same
exhibitor.
Awarded 1928 to Mr. Jos. Cockbain.
Awarded 1929 to Mr. W. Rawling.
Awarded 1930 to Mr. J. Rawling.
Awarded 1931 to Mr. J. Richardson.
Awarded 1934 Mr J. Rawling

Loweswater Show Catalogue,
1935: Mrs Heelis gives a cup for
Herdwick Sheep.

quite proud of her habit of dressing like an old farm hand, and not displaying
her wealth.

After she died on 22 December 1943, Mr Storey was having his Christmas dinner when Mr Heelis walked into his house. 'He said, "Here's the ashes,
you'll know what to do with them." I'd promised her I'd scatter them. Nobody
else was to know the place, not even her husband. We'd discussed it several
times. I talked to her the night before she died.

'So I got up from my dinner and went off and scattered them in the
place she'd chosen. I've never told anybody where the place is. She wasn't
daft. She knew folks would go and look at the place if they knew. I was sorry
when she died. She was a good woman. I intend to tell my son the place
before I died, so there will always be someone who knows.'

Hill Top, Near Sawrey, is the number-one attraction for Potter fans. Beatrix Potter built an extension on the house for her tenant farmer, but kept the original seventeenth-century building for her own use, although she never actually lived there.

Hill Top, which contains Beatrix Potter's furniture, is small and very popular, with 90,000 visitors going through it in the peak year of 1979. The National Trust now limits numbers allowed into the house at any one time, making no reductions for parties, not permitting coaches and usually shutting the house on Fridays. It must be one of the very few houses open to the public where they go to such lengths to restrict access. This means that there is often a long waiting time, especially in the school holidays. But oh, just breathe it in, stand in the porch, wander round the little garden, gaze in awe at the little rooms, furnished as they used to be, as seen in so many of her lovely watercolours.

*

For several years visitors to Hill Top were disappointed to find that the original watercolours from the Beatrix Potter books were not on show. Taken and hidden away, or so it seemed. Then they reappeared, and in a marvellous setting. The National Trust converted the original legal offices of William Heelis, BP's husband, in Hawkshead, and turned them into an excellent little gallery. It's fascinating to be able to compare the printed illustrations with the early sketches and paintings. A shame that the Trust has concentrated on Peter Rabbit et al., to the exclusion of Beatrix Potter's other watercolours, such as her flower paintings. (For her botanical watercolours, visit the Armitt collection in Ambleside – see page 135.) There's also a recreation of Mr Heelis's office, complete with his desk ledgers and period files.

*

Sawrey Village
Lake District

The World of Beatrix Potter, Windermere, situated in the Old Laundry, Crag Brow, in Bowness-on-Windermere, is a commercial creation, not in any way connected with Beatrix Potter. But it is one of Lakeland's most popular exhibitions, packing them in every day, all the year round. Just shows the pulling power of Beatrix. That film about her, *Miss Potter* (2006), has probably helped. The staging of the various tableaux from her books is smart and the nine-screen video show is very state of the art. See Peter Rabbit in his radish patch, Mrs Tiggy-Winkle in her cave, Jeremy Fisher in his pond. The video intro lasts five minutes, then you walk round the tableaux, finishing with a sixteen-minute film about her Beatrix's life. Foreign tourists love it. Superior Tate Gallery English types prefer Hill Top or the original watercolours at Hawkshead.

ARTHUR RANSOME (1884–1967)

Arthur Ransome was born in Leeds, where his father was a professor of history. The family regularly holidayed at Nibthwaite in the Lake District, and he was carried up to the top of Coniston Old Man as an infant. He went to a prep school in Windermere, then to Rugby School, before moving to London and becoming an essayist and journalist. He went to Russia in 1913 and became a correspondent for the *Observer* and other papers. During this time he fell in love with Evgenia Shelepina, secretary to Trotsky, so an excellent contact for any correspondent. He was already married, to Ivy, daughter of a Bournemouth solicitor, and had a daughter, but when his divorce eventually came through he married Evgenia in 1924. In 1925 they bought a house in Lakeland – the first of several they would occupy in the Lake District – at Low Ledderburn near Windermere.

In 1929 Ransome began his *Swallows and Amazons* series of children's books, twelve in all, of which five were set exclusively in Lakeland – *Swallows and Amazons*, *Swallowdale*, *Winter Holiday*, *Pigeon Post* and *The Picts and the Martyrs*. They reflected his own passions for sailing, camping and fishing, and were set around Coniston Water and Windermere. Ransome continued to

Sawrey, the village where Beatrix Potter lived.

sail into his seventies. He died in 1967 aged 83. He and his wife are both buried at Rusland in the Furness Fells. There is a room devoted to his life in the Museum of Lakeland Life at Abbot Hall in Kendal (see page 151).

SIR HUGH WALPOLE (1884–1941)

Hugh Walpole was born in New Zealand, where his father was a parish priest. He was sent to school in England and for a time was in Durham, where his father had been made principal of Bede College. He went to Cambridge, then became a book reviewer and journalist. Like Arthur Ransome – his exact contemporary – he was a war correspondent in the First World War, working for the *Daily Mail*.

In 1924, Walpole moved into a house near Keswick. His earnings from his books and writing, including Hollywood scripts, enabled him also to maintain his London flat in Piccadilly. But it was Brackenburn, on the slopes of Catbells overlooking Derwentwater (see page 64), that Walpole now regarded as his principal home. Walpole loved Cumbria: to this day there is a bench on the lower slopes of Catbells, with spectacular views across Derwentwater towards Skiddaw, with the inscription 'To the memory of Sir Hugh Walpole, CBE, of Brackenburn.' And his fiction – especially the four novels of the commercially successful Herries series, set among the Northern Fells – vividly evokes the scenery and atmosphere of the Lake District. *Rogue Herries* came out in 1930, *Judith Paris* in 1931, *The Fortress* in 1932 and *Vanessa* in 1933.

Walpole never married, but the year he moved to Derwentwater he met Harold Cheevers, who became his friend and companion and remained so for the rest of his life. Cheevers, a policeman with a wife and two children, left the police force to become Walpole's chauffeur. But he was probably rather more than that. Walpole placed great trust in Cheevers, who accompanied the novelist wherever he went, whether at Brackenburn or Piccadilly or on trips abroad. Their relationship was of course not known to the general public in his lifetime, and he was always terribly discreet, otherwise he would probably not have got knighted in 1937.

Good dog – Hugh Walpole with Bingo at Brackenburn, Derwentwater.

HUGH WALPOLE & HIS DOG "BINGO"

Walpole was also a notable art collector, owning works by Constable, Gainsborough, Turner, Utrillo, Manet, Picasso and Cézanne. He bequeathed a number of works to The Tate, including paintings by Cézanne, Renoir and Augustus John.

Today, his Herries books are remembered in Lakeland and written about from time to time; tourist-board persons point out where they were set and there is a constant talk of them being turned into major films, but nothing ever seems to happen, although *Rogue Herries* was adapted for the theatre and performed at Keswick's Theatre by the Lake in 2013. But mostly the thirty-six novels of Hugh Walpole gather dust in Lakeland charity shops.

ALFRED WAINWRIGHT (1907–91)

A. W., as he always referred to himself, never liking his Christian name, was born in a back-to-back house in Blackburn, the son of an itinerant and drunken stone mason. He left school at thirteen and become an office boy at the Town Hall. After long years of night school and correspondence class, he qualified as a municipal accountant.

His passion for the Lake District began on his first visit in 1930, looking down from Orrest Head over Windermere. From then on he vowed to somehow move to Lakeland, which he eventually managed in 1941, getting a job in the Borough Treasurer's department at Kendal, later becoming the Borough Treasurer.

He began his *Pictorial Guides* for himself, accounts of his climbs up all the Lakeland fells, illustrated by himself, which he would read by the fireside in his old age, but in 1955 he decided to self-publish them, believing no printer could do justice to his lettering and his artwork. Even the headlines and page numbers were all in his immaculate hand. His seven *Pictorial Guides* came out between 1955 and 1966 and are looked upon today by all Lakers as little masterpieces, works of art in themselves. He was following in some sense the guidebooks produced by the earlier Lakes writers, giving advice, suggesting routes to take, but it was unusual that he illustrated every page himself. He went on to write and illustrate over forty books, about Lakeland and also Scotland and Wales.

He had married Ruth, a local mill girl from Blackburn, and they had one child, a son called Peter, but the marriage had soon become unhappy, at least for A. W. He tried to suggest that she had somehow fallen behind socially and intellectually as he had climbed the professional ladder. He maintained that the marriage had collapsed in Lakeland because his wife could no longer stand the fact that he was putting all his physical energies, time and thought into walking the fells. The truth was more likely the other way around – he had thrown himself into the fells to escape his marriage and exhaust himself physically.

For years he had avoided all publicity, not revealing any details of himself on the dust jackets of his *Pictorial Guides*, or even if he was alive, but in his later years he was persuaded to appear on TV and write a series of coffee-table books about Lakeland – in order to make money for the animal charity that he and his second wife, Betty, were supporting.

His readers and the general public did not know for a long time that all his now-considerable income from his books was going to help animals. In fact, it came as a total surprise to me when I managed to interview him for my *Walk Around the Lakes* book in 1978.

A MEETING WITH WAINWRIGHT, 1978

I rather tricked him into seeing me. He never answers the telephone, which makes it hard, for a start, to get him. But one day I got his wife on the phone and she was kind enough to say that Wainwright knew my book on Hadrian's Wall and she was sure he would see me. I said I just wanted to talk to him about his own experiences in the Lakes and hear any advice he might give me. He agreed, on the condition that nothing ended up in any newspaper.

He's a very tall, well-built man of seventy-one with thick white hair and a soft Lancashire accent. He lives in a modern house in Kendal, which is rather suburban at the front, facing other houses in a cul-de-sac, but at the back it has fine, open views of the fells. The interior is modest and chintzy, with no sign of affluent living. There are a lot of cats around. He doesn't appear to be a reader, as there were only a few books, many of them presentation copies of books by other Lakes writers (which he admitted he hadn't yet read). The telephone rang constantly during the four hours I was with him and he never answered it once. His wife was out. If her friends ring and there's no answer, they know she's out and soon hang up.

Perhaps his best-known book, after the Lakeland fell guides, is his guide to the Pennine Way. This came out in 1968 and in ten years has sold 100,000 copies. At the end of it, in one of his usual little personal pieces, he said that whoever did the whole walk and got to the end at Kirk Yetholm could have a drink on him. Every year, the publican of the Border Hotel sends him a bill for the free pints he's given to Pennine Way walkers. Last year, Wainwright had to fork out £400. 'It's quite shocking the price of beer now. Back in 1968 beer was only 1s 6d a pint. Now it's four shillings! But I don't really regret the promise. If you've walked 270 miles, a free pint is a nice thing to have at the end.'

The day I was with him he'd just brought out another book: drawings of nineteenth-century Kendal. He'd based them on old photographs that had recently been discovered, glass negatives that were too worn to reproduce as photographs. That afternoon his wife was busy hanging his hundred or so originals in Abbot Hall Art Gallery, getting ready for an exhibition the next day. I went along later to see her and bought three of them — and to my surprise found I had to sign the cheque to 'Animal Rescue Cumbria'.

He considers he has quite enough for his own personal needs, from his local government pension and old age pension. Instead, he has devoted himself to helping animal charities.

From *A Walk Around the Lakes,* Hunter Davies, 1979

Lakeland Artists

GEORGE ROMNEY (1734–1802)

George Romney was born in Beckside in Dalton-in-Furness, the third son (of eleven children) of John Romney, cabinetmaker, and Anne Simpson. He was a poor student and so was apprenticed to his father's business at the age of eleven.

He proved to have a natural ability for drawing and making things from wood – including violins (which he played throughout his life). From the age of fifteen, he was taught art informally by a local watchmaker called John Williamson, but his studies began in earnest in 1755, when he went to Kendal at the age of twenty-one for a four-year apprenticeship with local artist Christopher Steele.

In October 1756, Romney married Mary Abbot, but the couple were immediately separated when he was called away to York on business by his employer. After a year, Steele eventually agreed to cancel the apprenticeship, at George's request, leaving the young artist – now father to a son – free to pursue his own career as a painter.

In 1762 he moved to London, leaving his wife and son behind, and eventually established himself as one of the most successful and fashionable portrait painters of the time – more fashionable even than his great rival, Sir Joshua Reynolds. It was probably thanks to Reynolds that Romney was never made a member of the Royal Academy. His portrait of William Pitt the Younger hangs in 10 Downing Street. He did about sixty portraits of Emma Hamilton, mistress of Nelson, with whom he appears to have become infatuated. Abbot Hall in Kendal has several of his works.

After nearly forty years in London he returned to his wife in Kendal. Throughout the separation, he maintained contact with his family and financially supported them, but they never lived with him. She nursed him during the remaining two years of his life until he died in November 1802. He was buried in the churchyard of St Mary's Parish Church, Dalton-in-Furness.

George Romney (1907–95), the American politician, is a kinsman, as is Mitt Romney (born 1947). Their ancestor Miles Romney was George Romney's first cousin.

PERCY KELLY (1918–93)

Percy Kelly was hardly known in Cumbria, let alone in the UK, for the simple reason that for most of his life he did not want to be known, did not want to sell or exhibit his paintings. It is only since his death that books have been written about him, exhibitions held, his work admired and collected, and his reputation as an important Cumbrian artist has grown. There are echoes of Lowry in some of his work and of Sheila Fell (see page 246) in his landscapes. He strikes some as a primitive – he did not go to art school until late in life – with his liking for empty roads, dry stone walls and harbours. A lot of his work was done in charcoal.

Kelly was born in Workington to an impoverished family, one of seven, and for almost twenty years worked for the Post Office around Cumbria, from 1934 to 1958 – with a break for war service – as a telegram boy and then a sub-postmaster. He had painted and drawn every day since his childhood, and his reputation was spread by word of mouth.

When the London dealer Andras Kalman drove up to the Lakes determined to buy twenty drawings, Kelly sent him home empty-handed. 'They are so important to me I could never sell them,' he wrote, adding, with typical arrogance, 'When they see the light of day they will diminish any drawings of this era.'

Collectors would arrive in hope and depart in dismay. Sometimes he'd relent, shake hands on a deal, then change his mind. 'I still possess ALL my early work and probably the BEST drawings and paintings,' he told a friend towards the end of his life. 'I would rather starve than let things go,' he said.

Kelly was a great letter writer, mainly to women, and illustrated almost all his letters with drawings and watercolours, usually of flowers and plants, which have since been collected in book form.

Waterfall of Lodore, Cumberland, by J. M. W. Turner

He had got married and had one son, but then in 1985 he announced he had become a woman. The cross-dressing had begun many years before, but then he changed his name by deed poll to Roberta Penelope and spent as much of his last eight years as he could in women's clothes.

SHEILA FELL (1931–79)

Sheila Fell achieved national recognition for her work when she was made a member of the Royal Academy in 1974, one of the few women to be so, but her main subject matter and inspiration was the Cumbrian landscape.

Born in Aspatria, she attended Carlisle College of Art and then Saint Martin's in London. She lived most of her adult life in London, but returned all the time to her native Cumbria. She was greatly encouraged when she was young by L. S. Lowry, who bought her paintings when she was still struggling, gave her an allowance of £3 a week and always called her Miss Fell.

Sheila Fell's paintings are loved and sought-after today by Cumbrians – they can now fetch as much as £25,000 – because they are seen as so evocative of the Lakeland hills. It was almost as if her surname had inspired her subject matter, not just the fact that she had been born and lived in sight of them.

I interviewed Sheila Fell for *The Sunday Times* in December 1979. She lived in a little studio flat in Redcliffe Square, Chelsea, at the top of the house, up miles of stone stairs. I wondered how someone so small and frail could lug up all those canvases and materials. She told me, 'I intend to live till 104. I've promised myself I will. It's what keeps me going when I worry if I'll ever have time to do all the paintings in my head.'

But before the interview appeared in *The Sunday Times*, Sheila Fell was dead, apparently after a dreadful accident. Her name was Fell. She painted fells. She died after she fell down those stone stairs.

J. M. W. TURNER (1775–1851)

Turner was not a Cumbrian artist, and never properly lived there, but his numerous Lake District paintings are some of the best-known images of

Lakeland. Like many artists of the time, brought up on the guidebooks that raved about the Picturesque Lake District, he did annual sketching tours in the summer, which he would work up into paintings over the winter.

In 1797 he did an extensive tour of Lakeland, covering 1,000 miles in eight weeks, though this also included some time on the Scottish borders. He started in August in Keswick in the rain, which did not put him off, as he was fascinated by dark skies and scurrying, menacing clouds. Eight weeks of clear blue sky would probably have made him pack up and go home. From Keswick he went to Lodore Falls, into Borrowdale, then Skiddaw, Crummock Water and Buttermere, Grasmere, Rydal, Coniston and into Furness, working all the time, producing scores of sketches – many of which ended up as paintings exhibited at the Royal Academy in 1798.

7

The Cumbrian Character. . .
and Some Cumbrian Characters

D'ye ken John Peel with his coat so grey?
D'ye ken John Peel at the break o' day?

TRADITIONAL

I ALWAYS SAY I AM A CUMBRIAN, BUT IT'S REALLY JUST A BOAST. I was born in Scotland, moved to Carlisle at four, then went back over the border again to Dumfries, and finally back to Carlisle where I then lived from the age of eleven. So Carlisle is my home town. People like to be from somewhere, to belong, and who would not want to say they were a Cumbrian?

But it's not quite correct in another sense, for I don't really have a true Cumbrian character.

My wife, however, *is* a true Cumbrian, in both senses. She was Cumbrian born and bred, with family on both sides going back generations, and she has a real Border name, Forster, whereas my surname is clearly Welsh, despite my being born in Scotland. What a mongrel.

The name Forster appears in Sir Walter Scott's 'Lochinvar', part of his epic poem *Marmion*: 'Forsters, Fenwicks and Musgraves, they rode and they ran.' I often say to my dear friend Melvyn, 'Oh, does the name Bragg appear in Sir Walter Scott, huh? Never spotted it.'

She is also very Cumbrian in character. When we are walking down the street and there is a hole in the road with a crowd around it, or some incident has attracted gapers, I immediately rush over to find out what's going on. My wife will turn back, or make a detour.

If I see someone I vaguely know on the other side of the road, I will wave, even shout if they haven't seen me, then go over. My dear wife will look the other way, pretend not to have noticed. If accosted by someone she knows head on, she will be polite and charming. Having been caught.

I am willing to tell friends and total strangers almost anything, whether I've been asked or not. Aged four, I am supposed to have stood at the front gate and told passers-by what my mother and father were doing.

My wife is very like her father, Arthur, who always warned, 'Say nowt.' This could be put down to his wartime years, when walls had ears; spies were everywhere, so best to give nothing away. But it's not, of course. It's a typical Cumbrian trait, going back centuries.

PREVIOUS SPREAD
A group of slaters taking a rest.

If asked about her health, how she feels, my wife will change the subject. Me, I can grind on for ages, show people my poorly knee, the funny bit of fungus on my elbow – what on earth can it be, look, what do you think?

If my wife is asked about her work, the book she is working on, again she will change the subject. She never reveals anything about her work, pretends she hasn't got any, she's just playing, and is not interested in talking about it, with anyone, friends or otherwise. It's private. Ask me what I am doing and I will say, 'How long have you got?' This often comes out as showing off, or so I am told by people close to me (okay, my dear wife), but I maintain that they asked me, and anyway what I am doing is jolly interesting – always is – so I am sure they want to know.

Cumbrians don't boast, don't show off, and they are suspicious of flash, noisy people who do. It's not a North versus South thing, or rural versus urban; it's just how they are. They are private people. They don't like to show they are nosy or curious. They don't ask direct questions the way I do.

They are suspicious, wary and cynical about other people's motives. Arthur would often shout at the TV when politicians or celebrities were spouting on: 'They just want publicity!'

Cumbrians don't go in much for enthusiasm, or overt excitement, feeling it is some sort of failure or weakness to display such emotions. And they hate to appear pushy or aggressive.

According to someone who has known me a long time (okay, the same person), I had my elbows out and was pushy even when I was at school. I totally deny this. My image of myself as a teenager, which I am determined to retain, is of someone shy, sensitive and nervous who didn't speak out. Alas, over the decades other people have made similar comments. I like to think what they really mean to say is that I am energetic and enthusiastic.

If it is true, as I have observed, that Cumbrians are private, suspicious and buttoned up, where did it come from?

Being near the Border, and therefore subject to invasions by Scots or disruptions from the border raiders (known as 'Reivers'), they learned to stay indoors. Living in a remote county, cut off from the mainstream, with folks very rarely moving away, they were always wary of newcomers.

These traits, and worse, have been observed for many years. A report in the *Carlisle Citizen* in 1830 said the citizens of Carlisle were 'possessed of low cunning but are often outwitted. They pride themselves on their feats of deception and will chuckle over the misfortunes of a person.'

Another, more recent commentator, Daniel Gray, has described some Cumbrian folk as being 'hell bent on avoiding eye contact with the rest of England'.

And on the plus side? They are stoical. I read somewhere that Cumbrians make the fewest visits to their doctor. So surely that's a good thing.

LAKELAND ACCENTS AND DIALECT WORDS

Although Lakeland is no longer split between the traditional counties of Cumberland, Westmorland and Lancashire, and lies entirely within Cumbria (since the creation of that county in 1974), in some ways Cumbrians are still divided. Those in North Cumbria look towards either Scotland or Newcastle for their cultural interests and connections – and in their accents you can often trace a Geordie or Scottish intonation. On the West Coast, they have tended to be more isolated and cut off over the centuries, hence their local accent has been retained for longer.

Inside Cumbria, there are around four different accents, identifiable only to long-term natives. Carlisle has its own accent and is very different from West Cumbria, just a few miles away. The rural accents of Cumbria are very different from the townies'. The North–South dividing line for accents is often said to be Dunmail Raise, just above Grasmere. Once you go up over that long hill and zoom down into the Grasmere Valley, there is a distinct change. In southern Lakeland, there is a distinct hint of Lancashire about the accent.

So there's not really one particular accent that outsiders can identify as being 'Cumbrian'. When a Cumbrian accent is called for on BBC Radio 4 they usually either come out sounding a bit Lancashire or just vaguely north-

A postcard of a Lakeland shepherd.

A LAKELAND SHEPHERD.

495.

ern. Melvyn Bragg is thought to have a Cumbrian accent. His accent is certainly distinctive, which some have put down more to adenoids, but over the decades the effects of Oxford and the BBC have knocked off the rough edges. Walk down the streets of Wigton and you would be hard pressed to meet anyone talking like Melvyn. Though he can do a good West Cumbrian accent, being a very good mimic. Beatrix Campbell, who can often be heard on the radio talking about social and feminist issues, has an incredibly strong accent, but it sounds to me more like a Lancashire accent than that of Carlisle, her hometown.

When I was growing up in Carlisle in the 1950s, we used words like 'cushty' – meaning good – which I assumed was purely Carlisle dialect, till I heard Del Boy on *Only Fools and Horses* use the same word. We called girls 'bewers', or it might have been 'buer', for I never saw the word written down. Food was 'scran'. A man or a bloke was a 'gadgy'. One of the most useful words was 'shan', a word that my wife and I still use to this day, which means roughly to feel embarrassment or shame. As a verb, it can be used transitively or intransitively. So you can be 'shanned to deeth', which means the shame happened to you, or you can shan someone. And it can be used as a noun as well as a verb. Our children, despite being brought up in London, often come out with Carlisle phrases we used long ago – despite the fact that, when I go round Carlisle today, I don't hear anyone using those words any more.

We also sometimes used the word 'marra', meaning mate, but I think this is an import from West Cumbria, where it is still used today in everyday street conversations.

＊

Local Cumbrian names for the ages and sex of sheep are still in common use. 'Yow' means ewe, 'gimmer' (another word with Old Norse origins) means a yearling, 'tup' means a male, 'hogg' is one of last year's lambs, 'twinter' is a two-year-old and 'trinter' a three-year-old.

Cumbrian farmers traditionally counted their sheep using a number system whose words derived from an ancient Celtic language. The numbers went all the way up to twenty, and they still get listed in old guidebooks. But in my experience farmers in their daily lives don't use these numbers any more – only people reciting dialect poems.

yan	teezar	yan–dick	yan-a-bumpit
tan	leezar	tan–dick	tan-a-bumpit
tether	catterah	tether–dick	tedera-bumpit
mether	horna	mether–dick	medera-bumpit
pimp	dick	bumpit	giggot

Even non-farming Cumbrians in a big town like Carlisle say 'yan' for one and 'yance' for once.

A shepherd with a Herdwick ewe, c. 1920.

There are many words still used by Cumbrian people in their daily lives to describe landscape features and which appear on maps of the area. Many of these words have Norse origins.

Beck stream
Blea blue
Fell mountain, open hill slopes
Force waterfall
Garth enclosure, field
Ghyll/gill narrow ravine, usually with a stream
Grange outlying farm belonging to a monastery
Hause narrow pass
Holm island
How small hill, mound
Intake land enclosed from waste
Kirk church
Mere lake, pool
Nab projecting spur
Nes headland, promontory
Pike sharp summit, peak
Scree loose stones, debris
Skarth gap in a ridge
Tarn small mountain lake
Thwaite clearing in a forest

FARMING FOLKLORE

I recently went to an auction at Mitchells in Cockermouth, one of their weekly domestic sales, full of clutter and boxes, bits and pieces, as opposed to their big catalogue sales where they have some rather more choice and expensive furniture and paintings.

I made a successful bid for two cardboard boxes of assorted letters, books and papers, having realised on a quick ratch through that they had all belonged to a local farmer in Loweswater, Dick Bell. I had little idea what exactly was in there, apart from the biggest item, a huge family Bible.

When I got the boxes home I immediately offered the Bible to a retired vicar who lives in Loweswater. He said, 'Oh no, not another family Bible. I get offered these about once a week.'

It is a whopper, beautifully bound, but takes up so much space, and I don't know where to keep it. But flicking through it I discovered it really was a family Bible with several pages, in copperplate handwriting, listing births of the Bell family going back 300 years. It has helped me understand the places and names mentioned in all the bills, tax forms, letters, invoices, contracts and other details which the family had carefully kept since about the 1770s, including dog licences. Did you know dog licences went back that far?

There was a homemade, stitched notebook in which for a hundred years all the sheep were listed – which day they were sheared, which day they were dipped and what mixture was used.

Some of the items were printed, such as a run of almanacs for the 1860s given out by the Royal Belfast Town and Country. I take that to have been some sort of insurance company that specialised in Cumbrian farmers. It lists the fairs being held each month in Cockermouth, Kendal, Penrith, Wigton and Appleby.

At the end, each almanac has jokes of a sort you might not see printed these days:

'Is there much water in the cistern, Biddy?' asked a gentleman of his Irish girl as she came up from the kitchen. 'It is full at the bottom, sir,' replied Biddy, 'but there's none at the top.'

But best of all among the treasures – and they are treasures to me, which I will keep safely for ever – is a commonplace book, a beautiful leather-bound notebook, in which members of the family, and presumably visitors, wrote out, in immaculate handwriting, sayings and words of wisdom, quotations and poems that had amused or impressed them. There are also drawings and cartoons, all carefully executed, with exquisite lettering and decorations. Many of the contributions are dated, and run from 1909 to 1919, yet there is no reference to the war, though politicians like Lloyd George are mentioned.

One running theme is sexist banter, from both sides, which clearly amused them and which they'd probably read in some magazine, heard in the music hall or been told in a pub and then written out:

Three Quickest Means to Transmit News:
1) Tel-e gram 2) Tel-ephone 3) Tel a woman.

The Arithmetic Of A Good Wife
She who ADDS to her husband's happiness
SUBTRACTS from his cares
MULTIPLIES his joys
DIVIDES his sorrows
Practises REDUCTION in the expenditure

Women have many faults
Men have but two
They seldom do what's right
And never say what's true.
If they seldom do what's right
And never say what's true
What precious fools you women are
To love them as you do.

'Laugh and the world laughs with you
Snore and you sleep alone.'

May you be happy all your life

Be someone's darling little wife
Have turkey every day for dinner
Which you don't deserve, you little sinner.

There is a long, carefully written-out 'Advertisement for a Cook', which looks genuine at first, saying she must have a large heart and a small appetite, then you realise it is all a joke. 'Must be able to cook everything except accounts. (The master attends to this.) No policeman allowed in the house, except in the event of burglars. No cold joints to be passed out of the back door, until they are old enough to walk out without assistance. . .'

I like to think of the Bell family, and other farming folk, carefully copying out their favourite aperçus, then passing them round for others to enjoy during the long, dark winter nights.

*

What of the natives? Most of the literary figures we met in Chapters 5 and 6 were well-bred, well-educated Southern types – apart from Wordsworth, of course – but over the centuries there have been many local characters, well known in their day, and still known and sung about in Cumbria today. Here are just a few of them, in order of their dates of birth.

PETER CROSTHWAITE (1735–1808)

Peter Crosthwaite, despite his humble, rural background (he was born on a farm in Dale Head, Thirlmere, and apprenticed as a weaver), turned himself into a marketing and publicity whizz, a self-promoter and entrepreneur and self-taught scientist. Not the sort of chap you normally associate with our humble, restrained Cumbrian folk. He did all of this in Keswick, attracting local fame, or notoriety, but not on the national stage. Just think what he might have achieved if he had moved to London.

He was most famous in Cumbria for the museum he opened in Keswick, which contained a Cabinet of Curiosities and a set of musical stones he gathered from Skiddaw and played like a xylophone – they can still be seen and heard in Keswick today. Crosthwaite was also a cartographer, producing one of the earliest maps of Lakeland. He styled himself 'Admiral of the Keswick Regatta, Keeper of the Museum, Guide, Pilot, Geographer and Hydrographer to the Nobility and Gentry'.

He was a tourist attraction in himself, and was mentioned in letters and diaries – not always to praise his self-promotions. He had running battles with opponents and rivals, including a fist fight with another Keswick museum keeper. It is interesting to realise just how extensive tourism must have been as early as the late eighteenth century, to enable him to make such a good living.

In 1800 he published a pamphlet that suggested lowering the level of Derwentwater by one inch, which would release 200 acres of land for farming,

Clydesdales ploughing at Loweswater, c. 1935.

which both Wordsworth and Coleridge thought was a good idea. He proposed a canal from Silloth on the Solway Coast to Keswick. He died in 1808 of apoplexy, presumably a stroke, but his museum continued for many decades, run by his son and then grandson.

Visiting his museum – which was not cheap to enter, costing one shilling – was part of the itinerary for most nineteenth-century Lakers doing the sights.

*

The young John Ruskin, aged only eleven (see also page 219), visited Crosthwaite's museum in 1830. He gave the place a mixed review. . .

25 June, Friday, Keswick
The next day being showry we went to the museum belonging to Mr Crosthwaite, son of the original founder. When we entered the first thing that saluted our ears was the sound of an Eolian harp, the second that of a tremendous gong, which filled the room with its most disagreeable noise. This instrument consists of a sort of iron plate pierced full of the smallest holes, which were almost invisible. When struck, the iron vibrates in a most wonderful manner. At one of the windows were two small heathen gods, most ludicrous figures, which the natives carve out of wood with their own hands. We saw a piece of the finest plumbago, from the Borrowdale mines, value £2–5. Also some wonderful petrifications of tropical plants, found in this country at the depth of between 50 and 60 feet underground, and a leaf of the prickly pear, 2 bamboo canes &c. There were several old manuscript books, written before printing was invented, there was an immense bone, rather more than 1 yard & ¾, said to be the rib of a man 21 feet high!! We saw a beautiful diamond beetle, in a glass. We also saw a very curious glass, which when we stood at a

certain distance from it, we appeared to shake hands with our own shadow. There was a set of musical stones, which Mr Crosthwaite played a tune on with a hammer, which were picked up on the bed of the River Greta. Also a pair of shoes, which were said to be identical to ones in which King Charles was beheaded. We were then shown the head of a New Zealand chief, & several other curiosities.

RICHARD WATSON, BISHOP OF LLANDAFF (1737–1816)

When researching a biography of Wordsworth and reading all his letters, I could not understand why there were so many references to the bishop of Llandaff. What on earth was Wordsworth doing, toddling down to Wales?

He wasn't, of course. The bishop was one of the smartest, cleverest, most versatile men of his age who managed to serve as a bishop of Llandaff for thirty-four years, with a large stipend, while living in Lakeland.

Richard Watson, Bishop of Llandaff.

Watson was a Cumbrian, born at Heversham near Milnthorpe, and from the local village school he went on to be a brilliant student at Trinity College, Cambridge, becoming a fellow and then professor of chemistry, without having any previous experience of the subject, but he mugged up enough to get himself elected a fellow of the Royal Society. He then abandoned chemistry for divinity and secured for himself a series of lucrative ecclesiastical posts, culminating in the see of Llandaff in Glamorgan. In thirty-four years, he only managed ten visits to Llandaff, leaving his clergy to run the diocesan business. He married well – a girl from Dalham Tower in Milnthorpe – and in 1788 was left money by a rich relation, enough to build himself a grand house at Calgarth Park on Windermere. He spent the rest of his life increasing his own ample fortune from writings and church appointments. At one time he had sixteen ecclesiastical posts, paying curates a pittance to do the real work. He lived the life of a landed squire – hunting, fishing, blasting rocks and also entertaining and charming everyone, including Wordsworth and Walter Scott, with his wit and intellect and hospitality. What an operator. He would have done well in any age.

JOHN PEEL (1777–1854)

Peel was a huntsman, who was born and lived in the Caldbeck area. He was a legend in his lifetime, if only a local one, for his passion for the hounds. He eloped with Mary of Uldale (whose mother had objected to them marrying) on his horse Binsey (named after a local fell), and they were wed at Gretna Green. Thereafter he devoted all his energies to hunting, often at the expense of his own family. Peel was a much more selfish, unattractive figure than his legend might suggest. The famous song which commemorates him, now the Cumbrian anthem and known throughout the English-speaking world, was never heard by Peel himself. The tune was a traditional one and the words, by his friend John Woodcock Graves, were put to the tune later, fifteen years after his death.

> D'ye ken John Peel with his coat so grey?
> D'ye ken John Peel at the break o' day?
> D'ye ken John Peel when he's far, far a-way,
> With his hounds and his horn in the morning?

His grave in Caldbeck churchyard (see page 166) is well worth a visit, unless the anti-bloodsports supporters have desecrated it again. To learn more about the colour of John Peel's coat, hurry to page 297.

MARY ROBINSON (1777–1837), THE MAID OF BUTTERMERE

Mary Robinson, the beautiful eighteen-year-old daughter of a Buttermere innkeeper, became known throughout the Lake District, attracting gapers from far and wide. It shows that some people could always become famous for being famous, without the need to appear in a reality TV show.

In 1802, one of those who turned up at the Fish Inn to gaze at her beauty was a young lordling calling himself the Honourable Alexander Augustus Hope MP. He proposed and married her, taking her off on a lavish spending spree all round Lakeland, travelling in his smart carriage, flashing his impres-

JOHN PEEL, THE FAMOUS CUMBERLAND HUNTSMAN. MARRIED AT THE BLACKSMITH'S SHOP, GRETNA GREEN. 35/28

sive visiting card. The marriage of the humble but celebrated local beauty to the brother of an earl (as he claimed) was widely reported, and Samuel Taylor Coleridge wrote in the London *Morning Post* of 'the romantic marriage'. Until the police caught up with Hope, that is. He turned out to be a con man and a bigamist called John Hatfield from the West Country who had left a string of broken hearts and fatherless children all over England.

He was tried at the assizes in Carlisle in 1803. Wordsworth, his sister Dorothy and Coleridge were all in court in Carlisle to listen to the proceedings. They asked to see Hatfield in his cell, but he agreed to see Wordsworth only. (It is thought he turned down Coleridge as Coleridge also came from the West Country and might well have recognised him, under another name.) Lots of juicy letters were read out in court from the women he had wronged. The whole nation was agog and, of course, on the side of poor Mary.

Hatfield was found guilty – and hanged. Not for bigamy but for franking his own letters and pretending to be a lord's son, thus getting his postage free, which was a capital offence at the time.

Even more tourists flocked to Buttermere hoping to see Mary – including Thomas De Quincey and Robert Southey, who both booked into her inn. Wordsworth later wrote about Mary in his long poem *The Prelude*. Coleridge also wrote about her. The saga even made the London stage with a musical based on her exploits. In 1987, Melvyn Bragg wrote a novel based on her story: *The Maid of Buttermere*.

Mary later married a farmer from Caldbeck, Richard Harrison, in 1807 and had four children. Her death in 1837 was mentioned in the Annual Register and she is buried in the churchyard at St Kentigern's Church at Caldbeck. She is next to the grave of John Peel – making it easy for those in search of noted Cumbrians to bag two memorials in one visit.

One of the people who remembered the Maid of Buttermere was John Dalton, the famous scientist, developer of the atomic theory. Not the sort of person you would expect to have gone gaping or celeb spotting, but it happened by chance, before she was famous:

A postcard of the famous Cumberland huntsman, John Peel.

I arrived wet and tired at Buttermere to find the inn full, but by dint of persuasion a room was found for me and Mary got out of bed and I got in – and right warm it was, I can tell thee.

So Dalton didn't in fact meet Mary in the flesh, but he did sleep in her bed – a story he was able to dine out on many years later.

JONATHAN DODGSON CARR (1806–84)

Jonathan Dodgson Carr was born in Kendal, the younger son of a Quaker grocer. In 1831 he walked to Carlisle, according to the family legend, to seek his fortune and opened a bread shop in Castle Street, opposite the Cathedral. It did well and in 1837 he opened the world's first ever factory for manufacturing biscuits in Caldewgate, Carlisle. Until then, biscuits had all been made by hand. His firm, Carr's of Carlisle, did so well that in 1841 they received a Royal Warrant, the first biscuit manufacturer to be honoured with the royal seal of approval. Jonathan Dodgson Carr made the most of the Royal Warrant, displaying it from then on in all his company's publicity and advertising.

In 1851 he secured the contract to supply biscuits to the refreshment rooms at the Great Exhibition in London. He created a special exhibition biscuit, which was first tried out in his family home, with all his children taking bites and giving their opinion. It doesn't appear, from the recipe, to have been much different from their other sweet biscuits of the time, but of course having the name 'Exhibition Biscuit' stamped on it made people want to try it.

The firm received some unexpected but wonderful publicity in 1879 at the battle of Rorke's Drift during the Anglo-Zulu war. A handful of English soldiers managed to hold off 300 Zulu warriors by building a barricade – made out of Carr's biscuit tins, as illustrated by various drawings in the London papers.

Today, biscuits are still made at the original Carr's factory in Carlisle, though it is now officially called McVitie's, and Carr's water biscuits are still well known throughout the world. Alas, the firm lost its Royal Warrant in 2012.

HENRY SCHNEIDER (1817–87)

Schneider was not a Cumbrian, but became known throughout Cumbria for his industrial empire and his affluent lifestyle. He was a Londoner, the family having arrived originally from Switzerland. He became a director of various mining companies and originally came to the Lakes partly on holiday, but also to look at mining opportunities. With three partners he set up the Furness Mining Company, looking for haematite ore. Progress was slow at first, but in 1850 they discovered 8 million tons of the finest ore. The invention of the Bessemer process revolutionised steelmaking, and Schneider and his company became one of the country's biggest steelmakers, with fourteen blast furnaces in the Furness area, turning Barrow into an industrial metropolis – which it has remained, more or less, thanks to its history of building submarines.

Schneider had a home in Ulverston with his first wife, who died in 1862. He then married again, the daughter of a vicar from Lancaster, and built for himself a magnificent house above Windermere on the Belfield estate – now a hotel. He travelled daily to work at his Barrow HQ down Windermere in his yacht, the *Esperance* – later used by Arthur Ransome as the model for Captain Flint's houseboat in *Swallows and Amazons*. On his yacht, Schneider was served each morning by a butler with a cooked breakfast on a silver salver. At the end of the lake, he transferred to his own private carriage on the Furness Railway, which he had founded. That's the sort of commuting most people would enjoy.

JOE BOWMAN (1850–1940)

Bowman, long-time huntsman of the Ullswater hounds, from 1879 to 1924, lived to the age of ninety. Smart hunting folks maintain he was a better breeder than John Peel, though he is remembered only in local Cumbrian hunting circles.

The Lowthers have been Cumbria's wealthiest family for most of the last 400 years. In more recent times the family has begun selling off some of its thousands of Lakeland acres to pay death duties. In 2014 they sold Blencathra, reportedly for £1.75 million. Not that you can do much with it, as it is still an open, public space.

At one time, the Lowthers were like feudal kings in Cumbria, lords of all they surveyed. Wordsworth's father worked for them and Wordsworth himself, having started off hating them, became very keen to have their patronage and friendship.

They were behind the industrial mining and shipping development of West Cumbria from the eighteenth century onwards. Throughout Cumbria today, you will still see references to the Lowther family in the names of streets, shops, cinemas and businesses.

It is the fifth earl, Hugh Cecil Lowther, who is the best known, or at least the most notorious. He unexpectedly inherited the title on the death of his older brother in 1882, aged only twenty-six. He inherited thousands of acres in Cumbria, both Lowther and Whitehaven castles, a large part of Carlton House Terrace in London and mineral rights all over Cumbria and on the West Coast under the Irish Sea. He was a lavish spender, as showy as possible.

He had affairs with Lillie Langtry and other actresses, some of which involved him in court cases, but he was mostly passionate about sport and gave his name to the famous Lonsdale Belt for boxing. He was also passionate about the colour yellow, and made all his servants wear yellow livery. The Automobile Association, for whom he was the first president, took their colour from him. To this day, Cumbrian Tories at election time always sport yellow, not blue as everywhere else.

In 1893 he entertained Kaiser Wilhelm of Germany at his home, Lowther Castle, where he had also entertained the kings of Italy and Portugal.

Lord Lonsdale's First World War recruiting poster – rotters and cowards need not apply.

ARE YOU A MAN
OR
ARE YOU A MOUSE?

Are you a man who will for ever be handed down to posterity as a Gallant Patriot,

OR

Are you to be handed down to posterity as a Rotter and Coward?

If you are a Man,

NOW

is your opportunity of proving it, and ENLIST at once and go to the nearest Recruiting Officer.

REMEMBER

if you can get 15, 30, or 60 of your Comrades to join, you can all ENLIST together, remain, train, and fight together.

THE COUNTIES—CUMBERLAND AND WESTMORLAND—HAVE

ALWAYS

BEEN CELEBRATED FOR THE FINEST MEN, THE GREATEST SPORTSMEN, AND THE BEST SOLDIERS.

NOW IS YOUR OPPORTUNITY OF PROVING IT.

HURRY UP!

Please take my humble Advice before it is too late.

THE COUNTRY HAS NEVER BEEN IN GREATER PERIL.

LONSDALE,
Lowther Castle.

R. SCOTT, PRINTER, "OBSERVER" OFFICE, PENRITH.

LAKELAND

Before the outbreak of the First World War, the Yellow Earl had his own army – well, at least his own battalion – known as the Lonsdales (technically the 11th Battalion, Border Regiment). He had tried to dress them all in hodden grey, the colour that Cumbrian hunting people like John Peel traditionally wore, but when the war started, he was forced to put them in khaki, like all the other soldiers.

In 1914, he created a recruiting poster, which appeared all over Cumbria, suggesting that those who did not join up would be seen as unpatriotic and, even worse, rotters and cowards. ARE YOU A MAN OR ARE YOU A MOUSE? was the headline on the poster.

*

Cumbria's aristocrats, such as the Lowthers, still have their roots, and their ancient piles, on the fringes of Lakeland, especially to the east, around the Eden Valley. That's where the Cumbrian nobs tend to hang out.

Lowther Castle, just across the River Lowther from the village of Askham, is not one of your ancient castles, but a nineteenth-century castellated mansion created to show off the power and status of the Lowther family. It was built by Robert Smirke for William Lowther, 1st earl of Lonsdale, between 1806 and 1814. Some of the stones used to build the castle came from Shap Abbey, a twelfth-century monastic house of the Premonstratensian order a few miles down the River Lowther (now a ruin, of course, but in a very nice setting).

J. M. W. Turner's painting of the castle, *Lowther Castle – Evening*, hangs in Bowes Museum. Wordsworth and Southey both visited the house, keeping in with the Lowthers, despite the fact that the family had been so horrid to Wordsworth's father. They both wrote poems in the visitors' book. This is Southey's little poetic homage:

Lowther! Have I beheld thy stately walls,
Thy pinnacles, and broad embattled brow,

Lowther Castle, Lakeland seat of the Earls of Lonsdale.

And hospitable halls.
The sun those widespread battlements shall crest,
And silent years unharming shall go by,
Till centuries in their course invest
Thy towers with sanctity.

The extravagant 5th earl of Lonsdale, the Yellow Earl, entertained lavishly and spent a fortune on the castle and its grounds. He did rather overspend, though, and in 1937 the castle was closed. During the Second World War it was used by a tank regiment. Its contents were removed in the late 1940s and the roof was removed in 1957. The shell is still owned by the Lowther Estate Trust, and at long last some imaginative and expensive work is being done to restore it to its former glory. The site is now open to the public, but it will probably take another decade or so to complete the restoration.

MILLICAN DALTON (1867–1947)

One of Lakeland's best-known eccentrics, and there have been a few, but for the first thirty years his life Millican Dalton was fairly normal. He was born in Nenthead near Alston, where his father was a mining agent, and educated at the Friends School in Wigton. The family then moved to London and Millican worked as an insurance clerk. Then, around the age of thirty, he gave up city life and went wild – or at least went out into the wild, firstly leading outdoor and climbing parties around Europe and the UK, giving out business cards that said 'Professor of Adventure, Camping Holidays, Mountain Rapid Shooting, Rafting, Hair-Breadth Escapes'. From then on he himself lived wild. In the summer he was mostly camping in Epping Forest and in the winters in a cave he created in Borrowdale. At the height of the war, in 1941–42, he spent the whole of that winter in his Borrowdale cave.

He made his own clothes out of leftover material, his own tents and his own raft on which he sailed – and sometimes slept – on Derwentwater. He had a fantasy of sailing his homemade raft all the way from Derwentwater to

A photograph of Scafell Pinnacle and the Professor's Chimney, taken by the Abraham Brothers.

the Solway, which of course in theory is possible, but he never got round to it. He gave out postcards of himself on the raft – these are now collectors' items. He wore shorts all the time, again homemade, maintaining that he had beaten Scouts founder Robert Baden-Powell to it. His shorts had a large patch of canvas stitched onto the bottom, thus providing a form of ground-sheet when he sat down.

Dalton was a Quaker and a vegetarian, and became something of a guru, preaching the virtues of the outdoor life. At a time when the sexes were divided for most sporting activities, he taught climbing to women as well as men. He was a pacifist and wrote to Churchill asking him to stop the war, but got no reply. Despite his hardy outdoor life, he lived into his eightieth year, dying in Amersham Hospital. Today he would be fronting his own TV series on the outdoor life and be the author of bestselling self-help books.

His cave in Borrowdale can still be seen. On the wall he scratched one of his slogans: 'DON'T WASTE WORRDS. JUMP TO CONCLUSIONS'. Apart from the misspelling of 'worrds', Dalton is thought to have made another mistake – missing out the word 'or' between the two sentences; in other words, he meant to say you should *not* jump to conclusions. I prefer to think that he meant what he wrote. I reckon conclusions should always be jumped to.

THE ABRAHAM BROTHERS

George (1871–1965) and his brother Ashley Abraham (1876–1951) were pioneering Lakeland and mountain photographers, based in Keswick. They somehow managed to cart their heavy Victorian camera equipment up every mountain and produced photographs that sold in their hundreds of thousands and have now become classic images. They also pioneered many routes and ascents up mountains in Wales and Scotland as well as in Lakeland, and are considered a vital part of the history of British climbing.

NORMAN NICHOLSON (1914–87)

A poet, playwright and writer who lived his whole life in Millom. He achieved national recognition when awarded the Queen's Medal for Poetry in 1977 and an OBE in 1981, but his main following, and interest in life, was in Cumbria. He's considered the best home-grown Cumbrian poet since Wordsworth.

There's an exhibition about Nicholson's life and work in the small and slightly overcrowded Folk Museum in Millom, on the north shore of the Duddon Estuary.

JOSS NAYLOR (born 1936)

A wonderful walker in his and our own lifetimes – Naylor was a fell runner (see also page 289) and Wastwater farmer, often known as the Iron Man or King of the Fells, with unbelievable records for stamina. To celebrate his sixtieth birthday he ran up 60 summits, each over 2,500 feet high, non-stop, covering 100 miles and 40,000 feet of ascent.

EDDIE STOBART (1954–2011)

The creator of one of the biggest, best-known and, yes, best-loved haulage firms in the UK. He was always known as Edward, not Eddie. It was his father Eddie who in fact began the firm, but at that time it was simply a small-time local agricultural contractor in the village of Hesket Newmarket (see page 169). It was young Edward who turned it into a lorry leviathan.

Edward Stobart was uncharismatic, in that he disliked talking, appearing in public and meeting new people, had a stammer and avoided social engagements. Yet he went on to create one of the most charismatic brands, recognised everywhere and smiled at with affection.

In 1976 he first moved into Carlisle from Hesket Newmarket, leaving his dad with the agricultural business. His first premises were in Greystone Road, not far from Brunton Park, the world-famous home of Carlisle United. (I always say that, just to annoy my London friends.)

Brunton Park gates were pretty high, as it was only a year since they had been in the First Division, and Edward used to make a few bob by letting out space in his yard for fans to park their cars – enough to buy his staff cornflakes and chips. The staff at the time consisted of only two, both of whom he had brought with him from Hesket.

In 1980 they moved to brand-new premises at Kingstown, right beside the M6. Edward was quick to realise the potential of this location, as it put his little fleet of lorries right at the heart of the UK's transport system. By 2001 he had 1,000 vehicles, 2,200 staff and 27 depots all over the UK.

One of the secrets of his success was having spotless lorries, with his drivers in collars and ties, and giving every lorry a female name – the first of which was Twiggy, after the 1960s model, whom he fancied.

The Eddie Stobart Fan Club, at one time 25,000-strong, came about by chance, as Edward did not go in for fancy things like marketing and publicity. Families had started spotting his lorries and their names while driving on the motorways, and encouraged their children to write down the names. They then started writing in for a complete list. They got a duplicated list at first, which then grew into a printed magazine.

There was, in theory, no logic to forming a club, nothing in it for the firm. Members of the public spotting an Eddie lorry were not going to think, 'Hey, that reminds me, I must hire a 100-foot lorry for next weekend.' His business was with the trade, such as Metal Box, and then supermarkets, not the ordinary public. But it was the Fan Club that turned Eddie Stobart into one of the most recognised names in the land.

I had been fascinated by Eddie Stobart's success for some years, wondering how he had done it. I knew Hesket Newmarket well and what a quiet, rural village it is. I followed his exploits in Kingstown, then his conquering of the motorways. When I eventually met him, back in 2000, I could hardly believe that this shy, reclusive person had created such a massive business empire. I wanted to know the whole story, so I suggested to him that I write about it. I saw it purely as an in-house book, to be self-published by the firm, to give to his staff and business contacts – and perhaps to sell to the Fan Club. It was agreed, and that he would pay me to do it.

After a few weeks of research, I decided it deserved a national audience and possibly a national publisher. I sent a blurb to HarperCollins and, blow me, one of their editors, Val Hudson, caught the train immediately from London to Loweswater. Okay, there's no train all the way, but she came as quick as she could.

We walked round Crummock Water and did the deal. Val offered me twice what Edward was going to pay me, so I told him to keep his money. In the end we sold about 100,000 copies, counting the paperback, and won a business book prize from the *Financial Times*.

Edward died in 2011, aged only 56. Three days after the tragic news, Carlisle United happened to be appearing at Wembley for the Johnstone's Paint Trophy final – wearing on their shirts the name of their sponsor: Eddie Stobart Ltd. The firm was Carlisle United's shirt sponsor from 1995 to 2014, sticking with them as they dropped through the leagues. Yet Edward was never a football fan.

'I never went as a boy. I came from a very religious family and going to football was something you didn't do. But when we were at Greystone Road, I used to watch granddads, dads and sons all walking to the match. I think football does keep families together.

'I never did it for publicity, like Walkers crisps with Leicester City. I did it for Carlisle. A city like Carlisle needs a league club.'

8

A Miscellaneous Lakeland
A to Z

Can you direct me to the Beatrix Potteries?

QUESTION RUMOURED TO HAVE BEEN ASKED
AT A LAKELAND TOURIST INFORMATION CENTRE

A
ND NOW FOR SOME THINGS I HAVE NOT BEEN ABLE TO
fit in elsewhere, but which I think it is fun to include, as well as
amusing, surprising – and perhaps even informative – for residents
of Lakeland and visitors alike.

AGRICULTURAL AND SPORTING SHOWS

There are several dozen sporting and farming shows held every year in the
various Cumbrian towns and villages – all worth going to – and most of
them include native Cumbrian sports. They are usually listed in the local
papers or noticeboards. The smaller village shows, despite not attracting the
large crowds or having an extensive programme, all have a flavour of their
own.

The two big sports days are held at Grasmere and Ambleside. All Lakeland lovers should try to attend at least one of them.

*

PREVIOUS SPREAD
Wrestling at Grasmere Sports:
Hexham Clarke and George
Steadman have a go in 1900.

RIGHT
A photograph of Grasmere
Sports in 1911.

OPPOSITE
The Grasmere Sports
Programme, 20 August 1925.

Loweswater and Brackenthwaite
Agricultural Society.

CATALOGUE

OF THE

ANNUAL SHOW

In Field adjoining
Buttermere~Scale Hill Road End
(on 'Bus Route),

ON

Thursday, Sept. 12, 1935

Catalogues, One Shilling.

SECRETARY—J. N. ROBINSON,
STREETGATE, LAMPLUGH

"Times" Printing Works, South Street, Cockermouth.

Grasmere Sports is traditionally held on the last Sunday of August. It has been a major Lakeland sporting event since 1868, and has taken place every year since then, except during the two World Wars. It attracts up to 10,000 spectators, and is held in the 'ring' – the field just outside Grasmere, across the A591 from Town End and Dove Cottage. It's a brilliant location for the show, which features all the usual running, throwing and cycling events, attracting professionals from all over the country, along with the best of the traditional local events, such as Cumberland and Westmorland wrestling, the famous Guides Race and hound trailing (see pages 297–300). In addition, there is a contest for the best costume worn by the wrestlers. Grasmere Sports gets very, very crowded, so go early.

Some years there are mutterings about introducing such modern horrors as bouncy castles to appeal to the kiddies. But, at heart, Grasmere Sports is still a traditional Cumbrian show, administered mainly by Grasmere people.

*

Ambleside Sports is held on the Thursday before the first Monday in August, and is held in Rydal Park, just north of Ambleside. The tradition of holding an annual sports day in Ambleside dates back to well before the First World War; in 1887 the sports included wrestling, a 100-yard flat race, a running high leap, putting the stone, hop, skip and jump, a hurdle race, a fell race, a running long leap and a potato race.

The sports were moribund for a while, but then revived again about forty years ago. Ambleside Sports is now one of the biggest events of its kind in the Lake District, with track events, fell races and Cumberland and Westmorland wrestling. It's an exciting event to go to, in a lovely fellside setting. Locals of course maintain that Ambleside Sports is now 'better' than Grasmere's.

*

Loweswater Show Catalogue,
12 September 1935.

It can be hard to tell the difference between an agricultural show and a sports day, because they tend to overlap, but really, any event held out in the open on the Lakeland fells and fields is worth going to, if just to poke around inside all the tents, watch the animals running around yelping and prize sheep being paraded and locals with their weathered faces heading for the beer tents – plus the county quality in their Barbour jackets and Hunter wellies.

Other shows that are highly recommended are: the Cumberland Show, Carlisle and Westmoreland Show, Kendal, plus the ones at Skelton, Ennerdale, Eskdale, Keswick, Gosforth, Loweswater, Hawkshead and Wasdale.

BEST DRIVE IN ENGLAND

The Best Drive in England, according to a motoring poll, starts from Penrith. No, not into Lakeland, but the other way. It's the A686, through the Eden Valley and the market town of Alston, and on to Corbridge. Most of it *is* in Cumbria. So we can claim it.

BLACK MARKET

One of the best-known phrases in the English language is said to have a Lakeland origin. Graphite, or black wad as it was known, was first mined in Borrowdale in 1412, creating the pencil industry. By the eighteenth century, it had become so valuable that armed men guarded the mines to stop any being stolen. Wads of it always got out and were sold illegally in the back streets of Keswick and Cockermouth. Hence the expression 'the black market'.

CUMBERLAND AND WESTMORLAND WRESTLING

Cumberland and Westmorland wrestling is probably the best known of the Lake District's native sports. Wrestling began in Britain with Norsemen, according to legend, and at one time was widespread across the country. Eventually different parts of these islands adapted their own variations, but most of them have long since died out. Perhaps it was due to Cumbria being a remote county that it has continued here for so long.

What strikes most newcomers is that the men seem to be wearing old-fashioned long combinations with a bathing costume over them, or perhaps their underpants on the wrong way, the way John Major used to wear his, supposedly. And also these underpants seem to be heavily embroidered in a sort of, er, very girly way, like an antiquated sewing class that has gone wrong. Then, when they start locking horns, it looks like a trial of brute strength – but is actually quite technical.

It starts with two men facing each other in a small arena, watched by two judges and a referee. After shaking hands, the two men 'tak hod' – that is, lock arms – behind each other's backs. The aim is to try to topple the other fellow to the ground and break his hold. If both fall, the one on top is the winner. The secret lies in tempting your opponent into a position of apparent security and then quickly overbalancing him. To the casual spectator, the subtleties are often not very obvious, but the events, for boys, youths and men, usually have a sense of atmosphere and tradition, which make them well worth attending.

The best wrestlers usually follow in a family tradition and seem to be practically bred for it. Just like the best animals.

Cumberland and Westmorland wrestling is usually on the programme at most of the bigger sports events that are held in almost every village of any size or pretension over the summer. They are often billed as 'sports', like Grasmere Sports or Ambleside Sports, but mostly they are basically agricultural gatherings, with lots going on – events, displays, stalls, parades, as well as, of course, a variety of sporting sports.

CUMBERLAND SAUSAGES

One of the products of Cumberland known throughout the world – those curly, rope-like sausages that the butcher cuts to size, depending on whether you want to eat them or use them to climb a tree. Made from coarsely chopped pork and highly seasoned, they originated in Cumberland in the sixteenth century.

There was a local movement for some European law to make them a protected species, like champagne or Parma ham, as many so-called Cumberland sausages had become mass-produced and were made from pigs that had never seen Cumberland in their lives. They didn't quite attain that status, but in March 2011, Protected Geographical Indication (PGI) was granted to the name 'traditional Cumberland sausage'. To display the PGI mark, the sausage must be produced, processed and prepared in Cumbria and have a meat content of at least 80 per cent. It must include seasoning and be sold in a long coil. In Cumbria itself there are lots of specialist butchers producing the genuine article, such as Woodall's of Waberthwaite (in Eskdale, near Muncaster Castle).

A group of dry stone wallers, c. 1910.

The origins are said to go back to an ancient breed of Cumberland pig, which has now died out, or they could perhaps have been introduced by the Germans when they arrived as miners in the Borrowdale Valley, which would rather ruin their unique Cumberlandness.

DRY STONE WALLS

These are walls without mortar or cement, put together by hand, from natural stones and slates. A much harder art than it appears. Between 1750 and 1850, most of the open fells were enclosed or divided by these walls, even up to the mountaintops – an enormous undertaking, yet many of them still stand intact to this day.

You can have a go at doing it yourself at Brockhole, the National Park Visitor Centre on Windermere, or join a properly organised Dry Stone Walling Meet, which the National Park people run. You spend a day with a ranger, learning how to construct a dry stone wall. Most people turn up just to watch, then find themselves joining in. Not long ago, an elderly American lady joined in – wearing a white suit.

EGREMONT CRAB FAIR AND SPORTS

The Egremont Crab Fair and Sports, dating back to 1267 and held in the small town of Egremont, south of Whitehaven, on the third Saturday in September, is one of Cumbria's oldest and oddest annual events.

The fair begins when, at 12.30pm, about £40-worth of apples (crab apples, originally) are thrown to the public. A greasy pole is erected at dawn in the main street and a five-pound note placed on top. Anyone who can climb the pole can have the money. (The prize at the top of the pole used to be a half-sheep, but presumably that got too expensive.) There are track and field events and hound trails during the day. In the evening there is a pipe-smoking contest.

But the event for which the fair is most famous, and attracts foreign TV crews, is the World Gurning Championships. The entrants to this revered competition put their heads through a horse collar and grin or 'gurn' – the object being to pull a revolting expression; the most grotesque wins. Entrants with dentures tend to have an advantage here, though it is said that one year the contest was won by a sympathetic onlooker who was just watching.

FELL PONIES

Fell ponies are a distinctive feature of the Northern and Eastern Fells. Mostly black, brown or bay, they roam wild in groups round the open fellside and commons. In bad weather, they gather near villages or on minor roads. They appear to be completely wild, and are allowed to breed and wander freely, but they do have owners, so don't try to steal any. Formerly they pulled small

A pony and hay panniers, feeding sheep *c.* 1895.

farm carts or worked down the mines, and they are now very popular as children's ponies.

When we used to have a cottage out on the fells near Caldbeck, John Peel Farm, I always had to take care not to leave my car outside the front gate. The wild fell ponies loved looking over the gate to stare at our cottage, not aware that their bony, knobbly knees were pressing into the sides of my car. When I eventually sold the car, both sides were perforated, as if by bullets.

FELL RUNNING

Sports events usually finish with a fell race to the top of the nearest fell, often a gruelling 1,500-foot struggle, round a flag at the summit, then a breakneck dash back down into the arena. A straightforward, though torturous, race. At Grasmere Sports, they call it the 'Guides Race', though it has nothing to do with Boy Scouts and Brownies. It can be quite spectacular and exciting to watch.

All through the year, there are also lots of individual races up and down fells, with participants trying to set records for speed or endurance or the number of fells climbed.

One of the best-known fell-running events is the Bob Graham Round – seventy-two miles, forty-two peaks, 27,000 feet of ascent. It's supposed to be completed in twenty-four hours, though only 50 per cent of challengers manage this. The event is named after Bob Graham, a Keswick guest-house proprietor, who on 12–13 June 1932 broke the fell-running record by running up forty-two fells in just twenty-four hours. Hundreds of individuals have bettered Graham's achievement since then, bagging even more peaks in the allotted twenty-four-hour period.

FIELD NAMES

When we first acquired our house at Loweswater and its five fields, I used to walk around in the evening, look at all the trees and hedges, stand back and say, 'Goodness, you do look well.'

I would bend down to examine the blades of grass and say, 'I own you, every one, and love you all.' I would examine the broken-down dry stone walls and say, 'Don't worry, pet, I will make you better soon.' Which I did. To the nettles and thistles I would say, 'Gerroff, this is my land. Take your nasty roots elsewhere.' Oh the pride of ownership. It can get a bit soppy, not to say ridiculous.

I think back to the farmers and families over the centuries who have lived and worked here, tended the fields so lovingly. 'Don't worry,' I say to *my* fields. 'I will look after you, er, whatever your name is.'

The strange thing is, until recently it never really struck me that every field must have a name. Yet a farmer has to call them something, if just in his head, as he goes about his business. So I asked Richard, the farmer who looks after *my* fields, what he calls them.

My biggest field, furthest away, is the one I am proudest of. I have a fantasy of the World Cup final being played there, or possibly a Carlisle United Reserves game, as it is so flat and lush and gorgeous. Richard calls it Muncaster House Field, as it is beside Muncaster House, which has been named on local maps for at least 200 years.

Next to it is Pond Field. That confused me at first. It doesn't have a pond, but at certain times in the winter there is a hollow bit, which fills up with water and attracts ducks. Personally, I call it a tarn – *my* tarn – even though it exists for only a few weeks a year. Calling it Pond Field I think rather diminishes it.

The field to the near side of it, divided by the rebuilt dry stone wall, Richard calls, rather prosaically, Back Pond. He sees Pond Field and Back Pond as one field – which I stoutly disapprove of. I like to think I own five fields, not four.

Down the side, he calls that field Behind Joan's. Joan, now alas deceased, was the widow of the vicar of Loweswater and we bought our house and fields from her. Lastly there is Orchard Field – the reason for which you can guess, being clever.

An 1874 advertisement for land for sale near Appleby. Heelis, the solicitors handling the sale, was the family Beatrix Potter would later marry into.

Freehold Land
AT BRAMPTON,
Near APPLEBY, for Sale.

TO BE SOLD

BY AUCTION,
BY MR. JOHN RICHARDSON,
At the Masons Arms Inn, Long Marton,

In the County of Westmorland,

On FRIDAY the 2nd. OCTOBER, 1874,

AT 5 O'CLOCK IN THE AFTERNOON,

Subject to such Conditions as will be then declared,

ALL THOSE

Two Arable Closes

OR INCLOSURES OF

LAND

Called COURT WALLS, containing

EIGHT ACRES

more or less, situate at BROOM, in the Parish of Long Marton
aforesaid.

The Premises may be viewed on application to Mr. THOS.
STRONG, the tenant, and further information obtained at the
Office of Mr. EDWARD HEELIS, Solicitor, Appleby.

Appleby, 14th. September, 1874.

W. BARNES, PRINTER, APPLEBY.

Richard farms lots of other surrounding fields, one of which, leading down to the River Cocker, is called Gully Holme. He thinks the name is at least 300 years old, as he has seen it written on ancient maps.

So, as you stare out from the tops of the Lakeland fells at all things lovely, do remember that every field you can see below, hundreds of them, all looking much the same, has each got its own, individual name.

*

What about animals? Horses always have names and so do sheepdogs. Sheep don't seem to have individual names, unless the farmer's children give them names as lambs – although most pedigree breeds of sheep and cattle do have

'Clipping Day' for a lucky group of Herdwicks, *c*. 1930.

names, which get registered; usually it's the name of the farm, then a Christian name. Hens have to go through their lives nameless, poor things, unless they are pets. Our pet tortoise is called Tortee. Not that she knows.

The naming of names, for animate and inanimate objects, is good. It shows love and care, not just possession, that we value all God's creatures and creations.

I think I'd better confess now that Hunter is not my real name. I was christened Edward Hunter, but was always called Hunter from birth. I never knew about the Edward bit till secondary school. The school nit nurse read out the name Edward and I looked around, thinking, 'Poor sod, who is that?' Turned out to be me. Today, I keep it very quiet.

HERB PUDDING

A Lakeland dish called Herb Pudding, which was very popular in the 1800s, could easily fit in to any colour magazine today. Most of the ingredients were home grown, or picked from hedgerows: leaves of young nettles and dandelions, blackcurrants and various flowers, plus chives, all chopped up with an onion and seasoned with salt and black pepper. Veal or some sort of meat would be added with a beaten egg and a cupful of oatmeal or barley. It was then all boiled in a bag or baked in a dish. Sounds scrumptious.

HERDWICK SHEEP

Herdwicks are a native Cumbrian breed, now considered worth conserving, and 99 per cent of those existing are in Lakeland. They are originally thought to have come from Spain some 400 years ago, when an Armada ship was wrecked on the Cumbrian coast. But others believe they have been here since Roman times. The lambs are born black, then slowly their wool turns grey. They retain white faces, and only the males have horns. They never get fat, and no wonder, given the lives they lead, out on the fells on their own for most of the year. They always go back to the exact spot where they were first put on the fells – their own 'heaf', as it is known in Cumbria. They are incredibly hardy and can survive for up to three days when stuck in snow by eating their own wool, sucking the oil out of it to keep themselves going. Their wool is pretty wiry and bristly, but it was vital in the early centuries of wool production when most of it was centred in Cumbria. In Shakespeare's *Henry IV, Part 1,* there is a reference to 'Kendal Green', which was a locally made cloth, known nationally.

Beatrix Potter loved Herdwicks and insisted that her shepherds kept them, even though by then their wool and meat were not commercially worth it.

In 2015, a Lakeland shepherd called James Rebanks, who specialised in Herdwicks and had built up a large Twitter following for his Herdy Shepherd site, published a book called *The Shepherd's Life*, which became a surprise bestseller, topping *The Sunday Times* bestseller list for many months and also selling huge numbers in the US.

THE HIRINGS

One of the common features of Lakeland, right up until the 1950s, was the Hirings, a sort of outdoor labour exchange or recruitment fair. They happened each year on set days, such as Michaelmas, when agricultural labourers or domestic servants lined up to be inspected by prospective employers. Once they had agreed a deal, and the wage, and the accommodation they would be provided with, hands would be shaken and that would be it – you were tied to that person and that farm or house for another year, till the next Hirings. Naturally, the system could be abused, on either side, with vulnerable young rural workers being taken advantage of, or the lazy and the sly worming their way into affluent homes.

This is an account of a hiring day at Kendal in around the middle of the nineteenth century:

A notice for the Martinmas Hiring fair in Cockermouth, 1951.

The street was well supplied with young men whose want of situation was indicated by a bit of straw, paper or leaf exhibited under their hat-band. The show of female servants at the Cross was unusually small and the demand much greater than the supply. The

Cockermouth
Martinmas Hiring

The Town's Police Clauses Act, 1847

In consequence of the above Hiring to be held at Cockermouth on Monday, the 12th day of NOVEMBER, 1951 the Urban District Council deem it necessary to make the following Regulations under the powers given to them by Section 21 of the Town's Police Clauses Act, 1847.

That between the hours of 11 a.m. on SUNDAY, the 11th day of NOVEMBER, 1951, and 10 a.m. on the following TUESDAY, no Carts, Carriages, Horses, Motors or Bicycles shall enter Main Street between Sullart Street and Castlegate.

The Council hereby prescribe as an alternative route Sullart Street, South Street, Lorton Street, Victoria Road and Kirkgate.

Any person committing a wilful breach of this Order renders himself (or herself) liable to a penalty of 40s.

Given under my hand this 6th day of OCTOBER, 1951.

E. JENNINGS,
Clerk of the Urban District Council.

BAILEY, PRINTER, COCKERMOUTH.

girls were all ages from thirteen to thirty, looking remarkably healthy and fully maintaining the compliment of the bonny lasses of Westmorland. Most of them were well dressed and exceedingly cheerful.

More good temper could not be wished than was exhibited betwixt buyers and sellers. The bargaining seemed to be on the same principle you see in a cattle market. A number of questions are asked as to age, family, last service, what they can do and wages. 'What do you want?' said a farmer to a girl that seemed left at last. 'Three guineas but say three pounds; I'll not take less.' 'Ye're four or five and twenty, ain't you?' 'Me!' was her tart reply. 'I am just turned sixteen.' One man boasting to his neighbour how well he had succeeded, observed, 'Aye, she is a fine lass, I ken the breed of her.' The girls showed great freedom in asking questions. 'Where is your house?' 'How many kye [cows] do you keep?' 'What is there to do?' One man thought he would secure his end and in answer to the last question said, 'Oh, we have nothing to do.' 'Then I'll not hire with you,' was the reply. In a few instances, the mothers were there setting off the claims of a good daughter. They would say, 'She is a lale (little) 'un but she is a good 'un.' 'Can you milk the kye?' cried a strapping farmer to a young woman. 'My wife is on her last legs and I will take you for good.' 'I can milk nin an' ye're auld enough to be my grandfather; I'm not gaun to hire for life just now,' replied the buxom wench.

Anyone familiar with the customs of our hiring fairs and the chaff and banter that goes on between those to hire and those hiring will recognise this as an accurate description, and we are bound to admit that this freedom and familiarity between those who are afterwards to hold the relation of master and servant are not good for either party.

Carlisle Diocesan Conference, August 1873.

Report in *Carleolensia*, 1873

HODDEN GREY

A type of undyed grey cloth, very hard wearing, mentioned in the John Peel song: 'D'ye ken John Peel with his coat so grey?' (see page 166). Peel's coat could well have been made from Herdwick wool. On no account make the mistake of singing 'coat so gay'. Tut, tut.

HOUND TRAILING

Hound trailing has been a favourite sport in Cumbria for more than a hundred years and probably originally derived from the method used by huntsmen to train foxhounds. It is really fox hunting without the fox. It's done in the summer offseason, so it's perfect for visitors to watch. From a starting point, a trail is set down by dragging an aniseed-soaked cloth over the fellside, making the course as difficult as possible by including fences, hedges, walls and a variety of terrain. For a fully-grown dog, the trail can be up to ten miles long and can take 25–45 minutes to complete.

After the scent has been laid, the hounds are released. They pick up the scent from the 'trailer', and then the whole pack rushes off into the hills. They might be out of sight until the finish, when they follow the trail back.

On a hunt day, you can always spot followers parked in little groups at the side of empty roads and lanes, and you wonder why they are there, but then you hear the disembodied baying of the hounds and all the drivers jump out of their cars, binoculars at the ready, and hang over the dry stone walls to watch the hounds tearing down the fells, jumping over walls, bursting through hedges.

The end is always exciting, even if you don't understand what is going on or can't identify any of the hounds. At the finishing line, where most followers gather along with the owners and the bookies with their colourful stands and large umbrellas, all seems quiet at first – then, suddenly, it's chaos and commotion as the leading hound is spotted. The owners shout and dance about, whistle and wave to coax their animals over the line. One reason, if not the main reason, why hound trailing still attracts large numbers is because

OVERLEAF
A pack of Patterdale Hounds, 1890.